THE BATTLE
OF
BRICE'S CROSSROADS

THE BATTLE
—OF—
BRICE'S CROSSROADS

STEWART L. BENNETT
SERIES EDITOR DOUGLAS W. BOSTICK

Charleston   London

THE
History
PRESS

Published by The History Press
Charleston, SC 29403
www.historypress.net

Cover image: *Brice's Crossroads*, by Rick Reeves, www.rickreevesstudio.com.

First published 2012

Manufactured in the United States

ISBN 978.1.60949.502.2

Library of Congress CIP data applied for.

Contents

Introduction and Acknowledgements   7

1. "Hold Forrest and as Much of the Enemy
   as You Can Over There"   11
2. "I Should Go On and Fight the Foe Wherever Found"   25
3. "The Critical Hour of the Battle"   41
4. "You Cannot Hurry Me or My Men Into This Fight"   59
5. "Everything Was Going to the Devil as Fast
   as It Possibly Could"   71
6. "Order Soon Gave Way to Confusion and Confusion to Panic"   83
7. "If Mr. Forrest Will Let Me Alone I Will Let Him Alone"   109

Appendix A. Union Order of Battle   127
Appendix B. Confederate Order of Battle   129
Notes   131
Bibliography   147
Index   153
About the Author   159

Introduction and Acknowledgements

I remember the first time I visited Brice's Crossroads. It was during an early morning a number of years ago. The dew was still on the ground, and I remember how quiet and peaceful the area was. There were and still are a small number of plaques describing a general overview of the battle in certain places along the roadside. This is unlike what you might find at larger, more popular battlefields. I walked upon the one acre that was then set aside for interpreting the battle, examined the hill that served as an anchor for the Union left wing and pondered the destruction around Tishomingo Creek. I realized this small battlefield played an incredible role in Mississippi, Southern and American history during that sweltering June day in 1864. The Battle of Brice's Crossroads is a story of courage. It is a story about winning against long odds, a story of the stinging torment of defeat and about two armies that shared the American spirit. It's also a tale of two generals and how their decisions determined their destinies. Although they did not know it at the time, the battle that they waged would leave an indelible mark upon the land and on generations to come. After researching the battle, I decided to complete a full-length narrative work dedicated only to this incredible battle. Edwin Bearss's *Forrest at Brice's Crossroads* interpreted the battle in narrative fashion; however, the bulk of his work covered other points of interest as well, especially the Battle of Tupelo. Bearss's work, however, served to pave the way for the rest of us to follow.

Today, I live close enough to visit Brice's Crossroads on a regular basis. Fortunately, the protected areas of the battlefield site have expanded tremendously. The preserved acreage of the battlefield is well over one thousand acres now, which shows that there are many who are interested in what happened here and understand the importance of its preservation. Not much has changed on the battlefield since that day I first visited, other than some new parking areas and a couple of interpretive trails. The ground still remains silent today except for a few occasional cars moving through the crossroads. Maybe that's the way it should be. Today, people can walk the fields were the 7th Tennessee and 18th Mississippi charged. We can also walk along the Union line and examine the cemetery where the 113th Illinois and other Union soldiers struggled to fight off the oncoming Confederate forces.

The field where Sturgis's wagon train sank to their axles is still a field, the ridge where the log cabin sat overlooking Tishomingo Creek remains silent, and part of the original Ripley-Guntown road is a walking path leading up to where the Samuel A. Agnew home once stood. Fortunately, the topography is almost identical to the time of the battle back in 1864. Many agree that this battlefield, like Pickett's Mill in northern Georgia, stands today as one of the most pristine battlefields of the American Civil War. It is my hope that more people will visit Brice's Crossroads and ponder the battle, the soldiers and the history of this great country as they walk these quiet areas where the sounds of war have long faded away.

It has been my intention to complete a work on the Battle of Brice's Crossroads that someone with general interest in the subject could read and understand what happened, why it happened and what the repercussions were. This includes how the battle affected the soldiers and the western theater of the war. This is also a detailed work for those who like to have a comprehensive study but without giving all of the intricate details of lesser movements. I have also tried to make this a work that the reader can take with him onto the Brice's Crossroads battlefield. It is my hope that this work will help the reader understand more about what happened and where it happened and better understand the topography of the land that encompassed this great battle.

In developing this work, I have examined the overall picture of the western theater during 1864. From this point we examine, in narrative fashion, the two commanders during the struggle in north Mississippi—Sturgis and Forrest—the march by both forces toward Brice's Crossroads and how this crossroads became the crux of the battle. The battle and its different stages from the cavalry fight, insertion of the Union infantry into the battle and the fight on White House Ridge near the Dr. Samuel Agnew home is also developed. We will end with the Union retreat to Hatchie Bottom, the battle's aftermath, the overall effect of the Battle of Brice's Crossroads on the citizens and what it meant to the bigger picture of the western theater of war. It is my hope that the reader will enjoy this work and, at one point, visit this incredible site to see for himself this piece of hallowed ground.

There were a number of people who were helpful in this endeavor whom I wish to thank. Dr. Steve Woodworth, as always, was very encouraging and served as a great advisor concerning some questions and certain details I had of the battle. In addition, I would like to thank Dr. Sharon Enzor, vice-president of academic affairs at Blue Mountain College, for her encouragement and understanding while I completed the manuscript; Nan Card, curator of manuscripts at the Rutherford B. Hayes Presidential Center, and Edwina Carpenter, director at Brice's Crossroads Visitors Center, for their help with sources, especially primary source materials; Dr. Derek Cash, director of library services, and his staff at Blue Mountain College, Russell Hall, Parker Hills, Sam Agnew, Jeff Ketchum and Ruth Thompson, who were also helpful with research and materials; Doug Bostick and his staff at The History Press for their help and patience and for allowing me the opportunity to play a part in this series of works on the various battles of the American Civil War. A special thank-you to my daughter, Emilee, for accompanying me to the battlefield and taking many photos that were used in this book. I appreciate my son, Nathan, for his inquisitive nature and positive attitude while on our many visits to Brice's Crossroads. Also, I am thankful to my wife, Kathy, for being patient while I completed this work. God has truly blessed me with a great family.

Chapter 1

"Hold Forrest and as Much of the Enemy as You Can Over There"

I t had been a difficult fight, but now First Lieutenant Thomas Cogley of the 7th Indiana Cavalry Volunteers could only watch and admit, "The entire army was now in total rout. The infantry was streaming by the wagons in the marsh, beyond the control of its officers, while shot and shell from the enemy's guns plunged through them. The scene that ensued beggars description."[1] The disaster that Cogley and his Union comrades encountered near a crossroads in north Mississippi was one they would remember for the rest of their lives. Yet long before the rifles fired and the cannons roared near the banks of Tishomingo Creek, the fires of a civil war had touched America.

The events of 1864 would prove pivotal in the overall outcome of the war, and the fight for Brice's Crossroads—or the Battle of Guntown, as Union soldiers recalled it—would play its part in the bigger picture of the war. This was also the year that Lincoln would put the military fortunes of the Union and its armies under the authority of Major General Ulysses S. Grant. Grant had proven his leadership after he successfully led his army to victory at Vicksburg. Later, his troops opened the Union supply line to Chattanooga, which helped break the siege of that great city. Soon after, his armies pushed Confederate forces, commanded by Confederate General Braxton Bragg, back down Missionary Ridge and into their winter camps around Dalton, Georgia.

President Abraham Lincoln finally found the general the Union needed. Due to Grant's successes, he received the rank of lieutenant general and was given command over all the Union armies. The urgency of the situation required Grant to lead from the eastern theater of the war. When he left the western theater, he chose his close friend Major General William T. Sherman to lead and oversee the work of the Union armies in that theater. As 1864 began, Grant devised a new plan for the Union armies in both theaters of war.[2] In the East, Grant, with Major General George Gordon Meade at the head of the Army of the Potomac, was to keep the Confederate Army of Northern Virginia under the command of Lieutenant General Robert E. Lee from sending any troops toward the West. Grant was also expected to defeat the Confederate army while driving toward the Confederate capital at Richmond, Virginia. In the West, Sherman was to take the battle to the Confederate Army of Tennessee, now under the command of Major General Joseph E. Johnston, and to keep Johnston from sending any help east to General Lee.[3]

According to Grant, Sherman's ultimate goal was to be the destruction of the Army of Tennessee, if possible, and capture Atlanta and hold it. However, Atlanta would become a greater focus for Sherman compared to destroying Johnston's army.[4] Atlanta was a major railroad hub for the South and specifically the western theater. By taking Atlanta,

Major General William T. Sherman. *Courtesy of the Library of Congress.*

Major General Joseph E. Johnston. *Courtesy of the Library of Congress.*

Sherman would sever Confederate rail lines between the two theaters of war, thus continuing to divide the Confederacy. In order to make these goals obtainable, Sherman needed a strong army and an excellent supply line. He had the army, or armies, as the case may be. Three armies made up the Union juggernaut in the West. The largest of the three was the Army of the Cumberland. Next in size were the Army of the Tennessee and, finally, the Army of the Ohio. Together, these armies totaled about 100,000 troops.[5]

It would be an incredible undertaking to defeat Johnston's army and take Atlanta. However, Sherman believed correctly that if it was to happen, he needed to focus on how to supply his armies throughout the campaign. Although Nashville was the main depot for Union supplies, it was still considered to be in hostile territory. The supply line north from Nashville to Louisville, Kentucky, and the route from the Cumberland River also had to be guarded by Union troops. To the south, the distance from Nashville to Chattanooga was about 136 miles. Adding to this was the fact that Sherman realized, "every foot of the way, especially the many bridges, trestles, and culverts, had to be strongly guarded against the acts of a local hostile population and of the enemy's cavalry."[6] This took valuable manpower away from Sherman's front line. Nashville held much of the Union army's needed supplies. As Sherman and his forces moved south from Chattanooga toward Atlanta, the realization of the need to leave soldiers along the supply line in order to protect it from Confederate raiders and cavalry became increasingly obvious. Sherman found that "then, of course, as we advanced into Georgia, it was manifest that we should have to repair the railroad, use it, and guard it likewise."[7] Damaging breaks on the Union supply line could cause lengthy delays in the Union army's movements and could ultimately cause disaster for Sherman and his march toward the Confederate army and Atlanta.

Two main problems faced Sherman as he examined his supply line. The first was that he was depending on a single railroad track line known as the Western and Atlantic for much of his army's supplies as they snaked toward Atlanta. Connect this line with that from Chattanooga north toward Nashville and then into Kentucky, and one quickly understood Sherman's concerns. This line was vulnerable to attack, which led to Sherman's second problem and, quite possibly, his most vexing: the fear of Confederate attack on this long, volatile supply line by Major General Nathan Bedford Forrest and his cavalry forces. While Sherman took into consideration the abilities and exploits of Confederate General John Hunt

Major General Nathan Bedford Forrest.
Courtesy of the Library of Congress.

Morgan,[8] no Confederate leader was more feared for destroying supply lines than Major General Forrest.

While Sherman contemplated his situation, Confederate President Jefferson Davis had plans of his own. Lee continued to command the Army of Northern Virginia in the eastern theater. However, in the West, Bragg had resigned from leading the Army of Tennessee after the Confederate debacle on Missionary Ridge. After much consideration, Davis selected General Joseph E. Johnston. Now it was Johnston's responsibility to stop Sherman and his armies from reaching Atlanta.[9] Although Johnston's army was smaller, he did have the benefit of fighting on the defensive in familiar territory. Johnston also understood that if he could get Confederate cavalry behind Sherman's armies and upon his supply line, maybe enough confusion and destruction might cause Sherman and his armies to turn back toward Chattanooga and beyond. Johnston knew just the man and the cavalry that could make this a reality. It was Johnston's hope that at one point in time, the administration would realize the need for employing Forrest and his cavalry to break Sherman's railroad communications, by which he could then be defeated.[10] Forrest was already known for some of his victories and exploits in the region. Yet it was anyone's guess how long it would take for the Confederate government to come to an understanding of the best way to use Forrest and his cavalry.

In May 1864, Confederate Major General Stephen Dill Lee had taken command of the department that encompassed Mississippi, Alabama, east Louisiana and western Tennessee. This included Confederate forces operating within this large domain, including Forrest and his cavalry.[11] Although Johnston was clamoring for Forrest's cavalry to strike Sherman's supply line in Tennessee, Lee had his own problems. It wasn't easy to just let Forrest and his men move off into central Tennessee. By doing so, it would leave north Mississippi's vast cornfields and important rail lines vulnerable to Union raids. Furthermore, this could hamper the supplies to Johnston's army, which depended on north Mississippi for much of its provisions. Also, Lee's fears of Mississippi's vulnerability only grew when realizing Alabama's possible susceptibility to Union raids. Selma and Montgomery, Alabama, held important machine shops, ordnance and ammunition stores. Union raids through these areas only added to Lee's apprehension if Forrest was allowed to leave the region.[12] However, Union raids were already being formed and were coming out of Memphis. These forces were moving on north Mississippi while Sherman continued to press Johnston ever closer to Atlanta. Something had to give.

Major General Stephen Dill Lee. *Courtesy of the Library of Congress.*

May 1864 proved to be a crucial month in the war as Union and Confederate forces jockeyed for position. Memphis would play a key role in the western theater for the Union army. Union forces held Memphis for much of the war, and now that city would play a crucial role in Sherman's Atlanta Campaign. Although Union Major General James B. McPherson was serving as the commander of the Army of the Tennessee and moving his army southward under Sherman, McPherson was also accountable for the District of West Tennessee, which included the city of Memphis. In Memphis could be found the Union headquarters for the District of West Tennessee. It was here that the district's commander, Major General S.A. Hurlbut, was stationed. Memphis had seen its share of Confederate raiding and officer infighting, so much so that Union leadership here would see and feel a change in Union organization. Under Special Orders No. 150, Hurlbut was relieved of duty. By May 2, Hurlbut had begun his departure, but not without his own general orders that showed an example of the infighting that was taking place in Memphis. These orders included a stinging retort that "it is to be expected that libel and slander will follow all who are intrusted with important commands, and I do not expect to be, nor have I been, an exception to the common fate." The district would now test a new commander, Major General Cadwallader C. Washburn.[13]

Not only did General Washburn receive command of the district, but he also needed to follow the bigger picture of what McPherson and Sherman were trying to accomplish with the Atlanta Campaign. On May 5, Sherman began the great campaign for Atlanta. Although Georgia was on Sherman's mind, the specter of Forrest loomed large in his thoughts as well. Sherman would later admit, "There was great danger, always in my mind, that Forrest would collect a heavy cavalry command in Mississippi, cross the Tennessee River, and break up our railroad below Nashville."[14] McPherson also worried of the mischief that Forrest might do. As early as May 1, McPherson worried about the fall of Decatur, Alabama. If Decatur was not protected and held by Union forces, McPherson

Major General Cadwallader C. Washburn.
Courtesy of the Library of Congress.

reasoned, "The enemy would undoubtedly hold it with a small force and throw quite a respectable force across the river into Florence and open communication with Forrest, thus endangering very seriously our communication and supplies." Sherman understood the threat but also realized, "We must risk something."[15]

However, Sherman didn't leave Forrest to chance, as his statement might have sounded. Instructions for a plan against Forrest that had already been developed by Sherman were being put into motion back in Memphis. As early as April 19, Sherman had communicated his plan: "Brig. Gen. S.D. Sturgis is in route for Memphis to assume command of all the cavalry in the vicinity, and to move out and attack Forrest wherever he can be found." Sherman was more blunt in his message to the chief of General Grant's staff, stating, "I have sent Sturgis down to take command of that cavalry and whip Forrest."[16] For Sherman, Brigadier General Samuel D. Sturgis was a good choice. Sturgis came with a background that included military leadership. His uncle was Brevet Captain William Sturgis, who was made famous by his death at Lundy's Lane during the War of 1812. No doubt his uncle's exploits helped move the young Sturgis's application along when he applied to West Point. Sturgis graduated in the famous class of 1846 that included such leaders as Thomas "Stonewall" Jackson, George Edward Pickett, Ambrose Powell Hill, Jesse Lee Reno, George B. McClellan and Dabney Maury.[17]

Once in military service, Sturgis proved his courage under fire during the War with Mexico, in which he was captured and held captive for eight days before the Battle of Buena Vista.[18] Later, he proved his daring and stamina during the Indian Wars, in which he chased an Apache Indian raiding party for three days nearly sixty miles a day and overpowered the Indians near Santa Fe.[19] However, his greatest test quite possibly happened while on the prairie.

In 1857, the buffalo herds were a thing of beauty and danger. Dabney Maury had witnessed the herds on one

Brigadier General Samuel D. Sturgis. *Courtesy of the Library of Congress.*

occasion and recalled, "Our first view of the buffalo was very exciting. There are thousands of them, and we were marching through them for three days, at thirty miles a day, and all day and all night the air resounded with their bellowing."[20] Out west and among the buffalo, Major John Sedgwick led the 1st Cavalry Regiment, with Sturgis as his second in command. As the regiment moved among the many buffalo, an incredible herd was sighted thundering down upon them just a couple of miles away. Sedgwick froze in his tracks. He turned to Sturgis, asking, "What'll we do?" Quickly, Sturgis replied, "Time is too precious for explanations now, Major...better turn the command over to me for a little while—I'll steer you through it." Sturgis received command and had the wagons corralled as quickly as possible behind the regiment. The troopers dismounted, formed ranks and grasped their rifles as they watched the wave of buffalo speeding toward them. The column's flanks were thrown out in an inverted V shape, with the apex of the line closest to the charging buffalo. Finally, Sturgis ordered the men to fire, thus splitting the wave to the left and right of the regiment. This continued for about a half hour until the rush had dissipated into a stream. The buffalo lay thick on the prairie in front of Sturgis and his men. The regiment had been saved. Afterward, Sturgis relinquished command back to Sedgwick.[21] Sturgis proved his skill and ability by acting well under pressure.

The American Civil War would test Sturgis's leadership on the battlefield. However, controversy seemed to follow him from the beginning. During the early part of the war, he found himself fighting in Missouri at Wilson's Creek. Here, Sturgis took command of the Union army after the death of its commander, Brigadier General Nathaniel Lyon, during the battle. Controversy swirled as Sturgis examined the situation at hand and decided to retreat from the field of battle. While a number of his officers disagreed with his decision, Sturgis believed that the lack of ammunition, wounding of key Union leadership and defeat of Union Colonel Franz Sigel's brigade made Sturgis's decision that much easier.[22] This decision would come back to haunt Sturgis as those who served under him remembered his actions. Soldiers such as Second Lieutenant Loyd H. Dillon of the 4th Iowa Cavalry, who was wounded at Wilson's Creek and, later, seriously wounded in action at Brice's Crossroads, recalled, "My grievance against Sturgis goes back to the Battle of Wilson Creek Mo. At the time Genl Lyon was killed. We had the Rebs whipped and we knew it but on Sturgis taking command we was ordered off the field to our surprise and still more to the Rebs surprise. Who were…of retreating themselves as I have been told by men who was in the fight on this side."[23]

Later, in Virginia, during the Second Battle of Manassas, Sturgis's negative claims to fame were his actions off the field of battle and his statement concerning the commander of the Union Army of Northern Virginia. When frustrated with what he believed to be a lack of organization with the railroads and not being able to move his men out as he had been ordered, Sturgis commandeered four trains and refused to let them move. Colonel Herman Haupt was in charge of the railroad movements at that time. After Haupt came in person and explained to Sturgis how his actions were being a detriment for sending troops to General John Pope, Sturgis barked, "I don't care for John Pope one pinch of owl dung!" He continued to repeat this until finally his chief of staff was counseled on the matter in order to get Sturgis to listen. Haupt recalled that the chief of staff "was successful at length in conveying the information that the telegram was not from General Pope but from General Halleck. 'Who did you say, General Halleck? Yes, I respect his authority. What does he say?' 'He says if you interfere with the railroads he will put you in arrest.' 'He does, does he? Well, then, take your d____d railroad!'" Haupt believed that Sturgis's little tirade might have interfered with about ten thousand Union soldiers entering the battle.

Although the idea of preferring charges and having Sturgis court-martialed was considered, in the end it was agreed that Sturgis was, according to Haupt, "not in his normal condition at the time, and was afterwards willing to carry out instructions and acknowledged that the delay had been his own fault, I let the matter drop."[24]

At the Battle of Fredericksburg, Sturgis was sitting on a campstool against the back of a brick barn while meeting with some of his officers, as the fight was raging before them. His brigade commander, General Edward Ferrero, "came in from the front, much excited." Ferrero explained that his command "was all cut up" and in no uncertain terms demanded to know "why in the ____ he did not send them re-inforcements." Sturgis answered, "Oh, I guess not, General; keep cool; take a little of this, lifting the canteen to his lips." At this point, a shot came through the barn and just over the head of Sturgis. Yet he didn't lower the canteen until he had finished his drink. He then handed the canteen to Ferrero and walked over to the side of the barn to see what was transpiring. He then told Colonel Sigfried, "Now is your time, Colonel; go in."[25] What was in the canteen is anyone's guess, but Sturgis appeared to be less concerned about the battle in front of him on this day than he should have been.

In 1863, Sturgis went west with the IX Corps. Although he had led commands in Tennessee and Mississippi that had proved to be uneventful, the capture or killing of the famous Confederate cavalryman Forrest could boost Sturgis's career and get him back on track.[26] Sherman was willing to give Sturgis this opportunity. Therefore, Sherman would reiterate his demand to Washburn on April 28: "Hold Forrest and as much of the enemy as you can over there, until we strike Johnston. This is quite as important as to whip him." He also explained that Washburn could not expect any help from east of the Tennessee River, as "we cannot spare it, but rely on your own command…don't let Forrest move about in that country as he has done."[27]

However, by April 24, General Washburn had already met with General Sturgis, and a plan had been set in motion that included an expected force from Sherman that would meet with Sturgis's forces in Tennessee. Washburn also asked for 1,000 to 2,000 men to be sent from Cairo, Illinois, just in case Forrest was able to "swoop down upon us here with his whole force…until Sturgis returns it might be a proper measure of prudence."[28] Apparently, the direct communication was found wanting between Memphis and Middle Tennessee, so much so that by the time Washburn received Sherman's communication concerning the fact that no help would be coming toward

Sturgis's position near Bolivar, Tennessee, it was too late to notify Sturgis. Regardless, Sturgis and his men had moved out through western Tennessee in search of Forrest. This operation included Colonel George E. Waring's cavalry division of 3,000 men with four mountain howitzers and six pieces of artillery; Colonel W.L. McMillen's infantry brigade of 2,000, including six pieces of artillery; and, finally, an infantry brigade of 1,400, including four artillery pieces.[29]

On April 29, McPherson explained to Washburn that while the troops adequate to force Forrest to fight or be driven from west Tennessee may not have been available in the Memphis area, Washburn was to pull any temporary troops needed from the District of Vicksburg. McPherson also explained that, under the order of Sherman, no Union commands would be forthcoming that were to be a cooperating force coming up the Tennessee River to help near Bolivar. McPherson repeated the main goal to Washburn concerning Forrest: "It is of the utmost importance, however, to keep his forces occupied, and prevent him from forming plans and combinations to cross the Tennessee River and break up the railroad communications in our rear."[30] Much had been put on the shoulders of the new district commander, and an even greater weight of responsibility was waiting for Sturgis. While Sherman marched south toward Atlanta, Sturgis was already moving from Memphis and toward his destiny, believing a Union force would meet him near Bolivar to help defeat Forrest. By the time McPherson explained that no forces would be on the way, Sturgis had already moved out on his mission.

Union leadership had good reason to worry about Forrest. Although Forrest had no military training, it became obvious to all rather quickly that he was a natural at war and a force to be reckoned with. He enlisted as a private in the 7th Tennessee Cavalry but soon after raised and equipped his own battalion of mounted troops, whereupon he was elected as its lieutenant colonel. From his leading a successful escape of his troops from Fort Donaldson; his hard fighting at Shiloh and Chickamauga; his raids through Tennessee; his successful pursuits of Union forces in Alabama; and culminating at this time with the controversial taking of Fort Pillow, Forrest and his cavalry had made themselves seem larger than life to many of the South and the Union armies who crossed them.[31]

In 1862, Forrest was awarded the rank of major general and later served with Major General Braxton Bragg and the Army of Tennessee during the Chickamauga Chattanooga Campaign of 1863. It was during this time that Forrest quarreled with Bragg due to past grievances that Forrest believed were intended to ruin him. To that end, Forrest abruptly entered the army commander's tent, stating to Bragg, "You may as well not issue any more orders to me, for I will not obey them, and I will hold you personally responsible for any further indignities you endeavor to inflict upon me. You have threatened to arrest me for not obeying your orders promptly. I dare you to do it, and I say to you that if you ever again try to interfere with me or cross my path it will be at the peril of your life."[32] Needless to say, Forrest received an independent command that would cover west Tennessee and north Mississippi. He would also be promoted to major general by the end of 1863.[33] While Forrest had his difficulties with some of his superiors, he was successful and got the positive results the Confederacy desperately needed. Although this caused him some angst with superiors, his aggressive demeanor in battle and high expectations of his officers and men led many to join his ranks. Although this had a grand effect on Forrest's troop strength and numbers, it was a detriment for other parts of the Confederate service. This would come back to haunt Forrest at a time when these troops were needed the most.

Much was expected of Sturgis as he moved out of Memphis on April 29. By May 1, Sturgis realized that he was not only at war with Forrest but also the weather. Sturgis complained to Washburn from Raleigh, Tennessee: "Owing to the heavy rains the roads were very bad, all the creeks being up and requiring bridges to be either repaired or rebuilt." The next day, he reported from Somerville, "Forrest has, beyond a doubt, a force of between 6,000 and 8,000." Regardless, Sturgis sent Colonel Kargé forward with seven hundred men and a section of artillery to Bolivar, Tennessee, as quickly as possible.[34] On this day, Kargé met up with Forrest and part of his forces at Bolivar. After fighting for two hours, Forrest's men had to abandon their entrenchments after dark. Upon leaving Bolivar, Forrest's men crossed the Hatchie River and burned the bridge. This started the long chase of Forrest's troops through Tennessee and into north Mississippi.[35]

While Sturgis continued his quest to find the Confederate cavalryman, by April 29, Forrest had received intelligence that Union forces were readying themselves from Memphis for a move on him and his forces. However, Forrest had also received orders from Lieutenant General Leonidas Polk on April 25, stating, "An officer from Richmond here on his way to Tupelo to inspect your command…proceed yourself immediately to Tupelo to meet him." Forrest would move out of Jackson by way of Bolivar and then toward Ripley, Mississippi, and finally on to Tupelo.[36]

In the meantime, contradictory statements from citizens concerning Forrest's movements stymied Sturgis. By the time Sturgis reached Ripley, he found that Forrest had been through the area at least two days before. In writing to Washburn on May 7, Sturgis blamed his failure to intercept Forrest on the Confederates being "abundantly supplied with forage he was enabled to travel night and day and thus elude our most strenuous exertions." Interestingly, he went on to claim, "I should have continued the pursuit had it not been for the utter and entire destitution of the country from Bolivar to Ripley, a distance of 40 miles." He also explained that his horses were starving from lack of sustenance and boldly predicted that "I should have not only failed to overtake Forrest but would have been compelled to abandon my artillery and a great many cavalry horses, as they could not have returned over that increased distance." After much consideration and with counsel from his officers, Sturgis "resolved to abandon the chase as hopeless." He ended his missive as if he had obtained his goal: "Though we could not catch the scoundrel we are at least rid of him, and that is something."[37] Private Edward L. Chatfield of the 113th Illinois Volunteer Infantry saw things the same as his commanding officer. On May 7, Chatfield wrote, "We were up at 2:30, had breakfast, and started on the march back to Memphis at 5:00. Forrest has got clear out of reach. Our cavalry's horses were played out for the want of feed. So we were forced to give up the chase."[38] The problem was that Sturgis had not obtained the goal Sherman had in mind.

Sherman had much to ponder during the first week of May. He had officially started what would be known throughout history as the Atlanta Campaign. He moved his troops against and around Johnston's Confederate forces near Dalton, Georgia, on the Rocky Face line. By May 13, Sherman's forces were attempting what he would be famously known for, a flanking movement. This flanking movement took the Union around the Confederates toward Resaca, thus erupting on May 14 into a two-day battle. The last thing Sherman wanted to have to worry about was Forrest. However, what greeted him from Sturgis's writing on May 13 was not what he longed to hear.

Sturgis began by stating, "My little campaign is over, and, I regret to say, Forrest is still at large." Sturgis explained his needs in order for success, much the same as he had done in his writing to Washburn, but added that he might have been able to trap Forrest "had a force been sent to co-operate with mine at Purdy." He further explained, "I regret very much that I could not have the pleasure of bringing you his hair, but he is too great a plunderer to fight anything like an equal force, and we have to be satisfied with driving him from the State." To drive his point home concerning his need for more troops, he finished by adding, "He may turn on your communications and I rather think he will, but see no way to prevent it from this point and with this force."[39]

Washburn had also communicated the same news to McPherson, adding, "He is no doubt on his way to attack some of your weak points." Washburn would go on to boast, "West Tennessee and Kentucky are now clear of any organized rebel force, and no place in this district is in any danger or in any way threatened." This could be considered good news had it been the original plan. Washburn and Sturgis were to make sure Forrest was kept away from Sherman's supply lines, yet both felt comfortable in the knowledge that their district had been cleared of Confederates and to issue a warning to their superiors that the enemy was most likely to attack Sherman's supply line. Interestingly, Washburn also added that a new expedition would be planned that would go into Mississippi.[40] McPherson would communicate with Washburn that he was, in fact, "gratified to know that Forrest has been driven out of West Tennessee and Kentucky" and agreed that "could we have sent a force to Purdy at the time Sturgis left Memphis, it would have been an excellent move…but the necessity of concentrating all our effective strength on this line, and preserving our communication to the rear prevented."[41] It was wise of Washburn to comment on the development of another expedition from Memphis, for McPherson also mentioned that he agreed to this new plan to strike Grenada. It could at least be seen that Washburn, if not Sturgis, was working toward the overall goal of attending to Forrest.

By May 15, 1864, Forrest had found himself in an administrative dilemma. He reported to Stephen D. Lee that he had "members of my command who are deserters or absentees from other commands" and that "some officers are here from infantry to identify and get their men." Quite possibly, these officers were from Johnston's Army of Tennessee, looking to refill their ranks for the front lines against Sherman's Union juggernaut in Georgia. Forrest continued, "Any attempt on the part of a few officers now here to recover their men will result in the loss of 800 or 900 men." He went on to request a suspension of this act for at least sixty days, but to no avail. The matter was decided, and on May 21, a total of 652 soldiers were called out and sent back to their original respective commands. By May 23, another 126 men found their own way around the situation by deserting the ranks. These men were probably expecting the same fate that had fallen on their comrades earlier.[42] Forrest had lost a total of 778 men. Regardless of the situation, Forrest would have to work with what he had.

Chapter 2

"I Should Go On and Fight the Foe Wherever Found"

Information from spies and local civilians played an important part in the war, and the area around Memphis was no exception. Washburn and Sturgis, as well as Forrest, used them, but a spy or local citizen's information was not always accurate, and oftentimes that was how spies and citizens intended it. As of May 16, Washburn had received word that Forrest was in Tupelo with a force of about 7,000, including another 3,500 less organized troops. By May 20, he wrote to Major General Canby that Forrest was at Corinth and Tupelo with 10,000 to 12,000 troops. Washburn requested more troops based on the idea that "should I move from here there would be nothing to prevent him, with his large mounted force, from coming down upon Memphis. I am absolutely powerless to assail him without more forces." By May 22, word had reached Washburn from Colonel George E. Waring Jr. that sources he used put Forrest's command at 15,000 troops. By May 25, Waring had warned Washburn that according to a scout, "The impression was that he would attack Memphis; that his order to go to Johnston had been countermanded and that he had 30,000 men."[43]

Various accounts came in from different places and from individuals of different class and standing that had some truth and, in other cases, information that could not be trusted. One such situation came from Waring and included, "An English gentleman from Holly Springs, just here, heard a letter read from the son of the lady with whom he boarded, and who is in Forrest's command; he said that Forrest was going to Tennessee and perhaps Kentucky." Also from Warring: "A man from Pocahontas reported that General Forrest on Tuesday was at Corinth, with his cavalry and a force of about 8,000 infantry, and was conscripting everything that could be called man."[44] While these reports could be questioned, it was the arrival of messages from a particular spy and those from McPherson and Canby that did the most to put Washburn in motion to try to find Forrest. A man named Moses was accepted as a reliable source. He believed, as of May 30, that Forrest and a number of his men were in route to Decatur, Alabama. True, Confederate troops were on the move, but toward Montevallo and not Decatur, and Forrest was not with them but in Corinth.[45] Also, on May 20, McPherson had written Washburn that all was going well in Georgia and that the Confederates had already been pushed back across the Etowah River. He reminded Washburn, "Keep the enemy occupied in your district and press him at all points as far as your force will allow." From Canby on May 27, troop numbers and movements were mentioned, with the emphasis that "the importance of keeping Sherman's communications open is of paramount necessity." Canby reiterated the goal on May 30.[46]

Regardless of whether the information was correct and reliable, Washburn believed that he had to do something about Forrest, and fast. Therefore, on May 31, he ordered Sturgis to move forward once again from Memphis. This time, Sturgis would have Waring's cavalry of 1,500, along with Winslow's cavalry, which numbered 1,800 and six pieces of artillery with Brigadier General Grierson to lead the command. Added to this force was Colonel William L. McMillen's brigade of 2,000, including Company E, First Illinois Artillery, four guns; section 14th Indiana Battery of two guns; and part of Colonel George B. Hoge's brigade and A.J. Smith's division of 1,600. Finally, Captain F.H. Chapman's four-gun battery was added, along with Colonel Edward Bouton's brigade of colored troops, which was 1,200 strong. The plan called for Sturgis and his men to march on Corinth and destroy all supplies that could not be carried away. They were then to march the infantry down toward Tupelo while the cavalry, which was also heading for Tupelo, would stay close to the railroad. The infantry were expected to destroy the railroad as they moved south. Once Sturgis and his men reached Tupelo and there was still no sign of Forrest, the cavalry and infantry were to move on Okolona, destroying the railroad as they went, with the cavalry going as far as Macon to destroy the railroad. From here, a section of cavalry would be detached that would continue on to Columbus and destroy any Confederate property that could be found in that place. After resting in

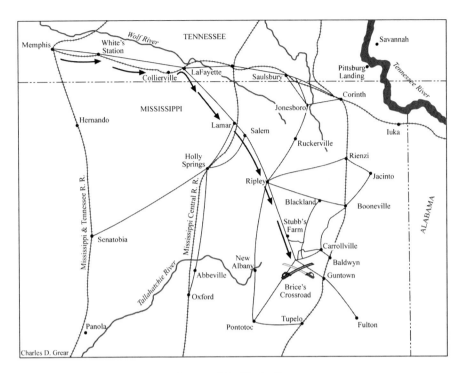

The area of Sturgis's expedition. *Courtesy of Dr. Charles Grear.*

Okolona, the Union infantry would then set out for and strike Grenada, with the cavalry meeting them in that locale. Once this was accomplished, the combined forces would, together, return to Memphis.[47]

A move such as this called for preparation and supplies. The wagon train that was to follow the expedition included 150,000 rations, including bread, coffee, sugar, salt and 75,000 rations of meat that was to last the expedition for twenty days. Washburn would add that Sturgis should "take your time; subsist on the country when you can. Do not scatter your forces any more than necessary." He then added, "This is a general outline, but you [may] vary as circumstances may require. The whereabouts of Forrest will, of course, have much to do in regulating your movements."[48] In other words, all the movements were important; however, the main goal was to find Forrest.

On June 1, the soldiers of the expedition moved along the Memphis and Charleston Railroad east to Lafayette, which was the easternmost distance the trains could run at that time. Once in Lafayette, it would be on to Corinth or after Forrest, depending on which came first. The evening of or near June 1 would find Sturgis back at Memphis at the

Gayoso House in one of his less-than-stellar moments as a commander. It was here that Colonel L.M. Ward of the 14th Wisconsin Infantry Volunteers heard Sturgis announce to other officers in attendance that he had received his marching orders.[49]

Ward also recalled that Sturgis acted as if he had been considerably under the influence of alcohol as well. Later in the evening, Colonel Ward recalled seeing Sturgis going down the stairs with another officer and stated, "From his manner and actions at the time I should say he was very much intoxicated." Ward went on to recall that after Sturgis came down the stairs, "he staggered up to the desk or counter, closed up the hotel register, raised it up over his shoulder, holding it for a moment as if he intended to strike his negro servant with it, then looked his servant in the face, laughed in a silly manner, and laid the book down again." Sturgis was then led outside by an officer who had taken him by the arm and out to the sidewalk in front of the Gayoso House. At that moment, a lady passed by, and according to Ward, "I saw General Sturgis take hold of her arm and detain her, and was apparently speaking to her, though I could not hear what he said. The last I saw of him he stood near the pillars with his arms over the lady's shoulder and around her waist, and the officer with him was trying to get the general to enter a hack that was standing near." Ward ended his account, "I became disgusted with the sight and did not wait to see any more."[50]

Brigadier General Benjamin H. Grierson remembered when Sturgis had entered Memphis back in April and recalled how his actions in Memphis were "not creditable to himself, nor reassuring to those who must be his subordinates—but, on the contrary, extremely discouraging." Grierson added, "Upon his arrival at Memphis, he put up at the Gayoso House, where, being dissipated in habits, he had a protracted drunken spree for nearly two weeks, during which he smashed looking glasses, crockery, and furniture to his heart's content, kicking up 'high jinks' generally, until his condition became notorious."[51] These scenes did not bode well for the expedition to come. Sturgis's actions had seriously hampered his credibility among

Brigadier General Benjamin H. Grierson. *Courtesy of the Library of Congress.*

subordinate officers. In this case, it included one officer in particular who was crucial to the expedition's success: Grierson.

While Washburn and Sturgis did not see Forrest during the last weeks of May, it didn't mean he was no longer in the district, as they had estimated. Forrest's own chief of artillery may have stated it best: "General Forrest at rest meant General Forrest studying the Federal moves and laying plans to sweep down upon them at some unexpected point and throw the whole machinery of war into confusion."[52] Like Union commander Washburn, Stephen D. Lee also felt the pains of command. For Lee, it included wondering where the Union army was going and why but also where to use Forrest for the best advantage. It caught Lee's attention when Union forces moved out earlier in May after Forrest and that these forces went as far as Ripley, Mississippi, before turning back.

Lee also felt the pressure to send Forrest into Middle Tennessee. Lee had planned to do so around May 17—at least until it was believed that a new threat was developing from Memphis. This time, according to Lee, the movement toward Tennessee was suspended "upon the advice of Gen. Forrest." However, when there appeared to be a delay in a Union movement from Memphis, it gave cause for Forrest to believe it was not to happen. Therefore, he wrote on May 29, "The time has arrived, if I can be spared and allowed 2,000 picked men from Buford's division… will attempt to cut enemies communication in Middle Tennessee."[53] Forrest received orders from Lee to move into Middle Tennessee with two thousand men of his own command and one thousand men from Brigadier General Roddey, who was commanding a division of cavalry in north Alabama. They would also take two batteries of artillery. The goal, according to Forrest, was "destroying the railroad from Nashville and breaking up the lines of communications connecting that point with Sherman's army in Northern Georgia." All was put into motion. Forrest gathered the needed troops and left Tupelo, Mississippi, on June 1. He even dispatched his aide-de-camp and Captain John G. Mann of the engineer department to make ready all needed particulars for crossing the Tennessee River. Forrest was at Russellville the morning of June 3, not far from the banks of the Tennessee River, when he received an urgent dispatch from Lee.[54]

For the Confederacy in Mississippi, it had become the tyranny of the urgent. While Forrest's mission was important, Lee could not ignore the emergency happening on his own front. Lee finally realized that Union troops were, indeed, "moving in force from Memphis in the direction of

Tupelo" and ordered Forrest to return immediately. The Tennessee River crossing would have to wait another day. Forrest moved out toward Tupelo and arrived June 5, whereupon he found that Sturgis and his command were to the west, only fifty miles away in the town of Salem.[55] Now that the Union forces were found, it was time to send out scouts, consolidate forces and communicate with Lee as to a plan for battle.

Lee and Forrest were not completely sure of the Union expedition's intentions. It could have been to destroy Forrest, his cavalry and the valuable crops of north Mississippi, or it could have been, as Lee considered, "that the column might be going by Corinth to reinforce Gen. Sherman in Georgia." Until they were sure, Confederate troops needed to be moved in order to prepare and meet for either possibility.[56] As Forrest focused on possible Union movements toward Corinth and Rienzi or southward around Baldwyn and Tupelo, Lee moved south toward Okolona. Here, Lee would gather troops and use Tupelo as a base if a battle were to form in that locale. Forrest would be able to call upon General Abraham Buford, together with Captain T.W. Rice's and Captain John Morton's batteries, and meet in Booneville. Booneville would be a perfect locale in which Forrest could watch the movements of the Union army and then discern what Sturgis's plans were. Sturgis's decision as to what road or roads to use would give away his intentions. In studying him, Forrest would then be able to discern Sturgis's movements and plans, thus allowing Forrest to combine his forces and strike quickly.[57]

Although the Union cavalry moved out of Memphis on June 1, Sturgis recalled receiving marching orders of May 31 on June 1 and thus left Memphis in the early morning of June 2. It wasn't until June 3 that Sturgis marched from the Lafayette area. Almost immediately, problems arose for the forlorn expedition. Administrative snafus in the procuring of forage for the horses caused delays. Forage was of high priority, especially since the wagon train included roughly "250 wagons, and a ten-gallon keg of whiskey." Wagon and train connections concerning the forage needed for the horses were confused, misunderstandings between quartermasters and the train conductor regarding the forage developed and even the weather refused to cooperate. Sturgis recalled, "A heavy rain occurred that day, rendering the movement of the forage difficult." The forage issue delayed Sturgis and his men at least a day. In the end, Sturgis found that "the quartermaster in Memphis was not in his office and could not get the communication until night, and all this time my wagons were waiting for it, and I was compelled to withdraw them without the forage in order to march in the morning." This decision would haunt Sturgis in the days to come. Not only were these demanding situations difficult to overcome, but when considering the men he was leading in the expedition, Sturgis would freely admit that "I had nothing to do whatever with its organization it was organized and sent out from here, and I assumed command of it near La Fayette, Tenn…I was an entire stranger to the troops and the organizations."[58] It would seem that Sturgis did not try to endear himself to his men when given the chance back in Memphis. Thomas S. Cogley of Company F, 7th Indiana Cavalry Volunteers, recalled such a chance for Sturgis when he reviewed the men from Indiana: "Contrary to the usual custom, he reviewed it, by riding in a cab, in front of the regiment. The most that could be seen of him was his prodigious black mustache, occasional glimpses of which were had through the windows of the cab. Derisive remarks about him were made by the men, before he was scarcely out of hearing." Furthermore, it was added, "On their return to camp, the men freely expressed their opinion, that under such a general the expedition would prove another failure."[59] This, too, would not serve Sturgis well, for in battle he would not know the history of certain leaders or regiments or they of him, nor did they feel any form of camaraderie with their overall commander.

Although Sturgis was unfamiliar with his troops, he did manage to organize them into two divisions under leadership they were familiar with. General Grierson was to command all the cavalry, and Colonel McMillen, who was the senior colonel and of the 95th Ohio Infantry, commanded the infantry. McMillen had problems of his own with the bottle. It was at Lafayette that DeWitt Thomas, colonel of the 93rd Indiana Infantry Volunteers, found McMillen, "whom I thought was intoxicated at the point where we disembarked from the cars…He was then commanding the First Brigade, to which my regiment was attached." McMillen was so bad off that he once fell when moving from the cars and had to be helped to his feet. Thomas was able to have him sent to a home "and place him in bed that night, and I took command of the brigade until the next morning."[60]

The order of march included "the First Brigade, with its artillery, in the advance, commanded by Colonel Wilkin, of the Ninth Minnesota; the Second Brigade, with its artillery, next commanded by Colonel Hoge, of the One hundred and thirteenth Illinois, and next the supply train, guarded by the Third Brigade, commanded by Colonel Bouton, of the Fifty-ninth U.S. Colored Troops." When it came to protecting the train, the following was true: "One regiment in the advance, one about the center, and one at the rear." As the expedition went farther into enemy territory, it would be changed by "adding a section of artillery to the rear of the train, and scattering two companies through the train. Each brigade was furnished with about thirty mounted men to be used at headquarters as orderlies, scouts, &c. The usual order of march of the cavalry was alternating by brigades and carrying their artillery and trains with them."[61]

Colonel Kargé of the 2nd New Jersey Cavalry led four hundred cavalrymen. These men of New Jersey proceeded to Ripley by rapid march with orders to destroy the railroad and Rebel property found within the area. At this time, Grierson and the rest of his command marched from Salem to Ruckersville. Here, Grierson waited for a day until the infantry and wagon train drew nearer. After sending patrols out toward the east past the Hatchie River, Grierson found that Corinth had been abandoned by Confederate troops, which had moved south. After examining the situation before him, Sturgis turned from moving his forces toward Corinth in favor of Ripley.[62]

By the evening of June 7, Union cavalry were in Ripley. It was here that the 4th Iowa Cavalry encountered Confederate resistance, thus pushing the Rebels through the town and about two miles south of Ripley. Confederates prepared a skirmish line on the crest of the hill, which could be reached by the road through crossing a bridge. However, this hill included the skirmish line and two pieces of artillery with a cover of woods. Although a heavy fire ensued, the 4th Iowa Cavalry could not break the line. The 7th Indiana Cavalry was brought forward at a trot and was ordered to assault the hill. The ground that the troops would cover was a "low creek bottom, cut up by ditches, and covered with logs and fallen timber. It was impossible to advance mounted." The men were dismounted and moved forward on foot. By this time, it was getting dark, and the men found themselves stumbling over logs and even falling into ditches. Upon reaching the hill, it was found that the Confederates had left. The Rebels had been flanked out of position, and not a shot was fired. Both sides had lived to die another day.[63]

On the evening of June 7 and the morning of June 8, a somewhat strange and possibly embarrassing scenario played out for Colonel Kargé and his men. During the morning, a courier managed to move through Confederate lines to report that the colonel was in a precarious situation. The 4th Missouri Cavalry and the 7th Indiana Cavalry were sent to Kargé's assistance. While leading his four hundred troopers, Kargé had "encountered the enemy beyond Ruckersville and was driven on an island in the Hatchie River, and surrounded." Fortunately, Kargé and his command were met along the road just beyond Ruckersville after he and his men "effected his escape by swimming his command across the river at a point not guarded. The two commands returned to Ripley."[64]

Sturgis's expedition had its share of problems from the moment it left Memphis. From June 1 until it reached Ripley, the rain fell every day. Edward Chatfield wrote on June 1, "We got on the cars and went out about 10 miles between La Fayette and La Grange, where we got off the cars and camped for the night. Rain began in the afternoon; it is raining hard now." Soldiers dealt with various trials and tribulations as they marched through north Mississippi in early June. John Wool Bartleson of the 81st Illinois Infantry Regiment bemoaned Sturgis and how "he kept us on short rations, with two men detailed each day to forage through the country for our mets. Through all the rain we had nothing to drink, not withstanding that plenty of whiskey had been taken on the wagon train to guard against fever and malaria." Taking the valuables of the area citizens was not beyond some of the soldiers. At one point during the march, it was believed that at least one Union soldier had entered and "ransacked" an elderly woman's home, possibly looking for clean, dry clothes. Bartleson recalled that the army had halted in the road near which was a double log farmhouse with a porch in front. "All at once I was attracted by the old lady, gray haired, about seventy-five years old. She was marching up and down the porch, praying so loud that all could hear her, that God would have vengeance upon us and destroy us all!" He added, "I felt very sorry for this old grand mother. Her prayer was answered, too, surely and speedily." Swamps were also a problem along the way, as the incessant rains continued to fall. Bartleson found that "some of the swamps were nearly impassible. At one mirey swamp we had to tear down a small church edifice to get timbers for a corduroy road across." He further added, "Officers and men cut off the lower part of their pant legs, so as to march more easily. We were a bedraggled army."[65]

It was difficult to find forage for the cavalry, much less for the horses and mules that drew the artillery and 250 wagons of needed supplies for the troops. Sturgis even began to question if the expedition should proceed, stating, "At Ripley it became a serious question in my mind as to whether or not I should proceed any further. The rain still fell in torrents. The artillery and wagons were literally mired down, and the starved and exhausted animals could with difficulty drag them along." It was at this point that Sturgis called together his division commanders and explained to them the way he saw the situation, including obstacles such as the great delay due to continuous rain, the bad condition of the roads, the exhausted condition of the animals and "the great probability that the enemy would avail himself of the time thus afforded him to concentrate an overwhelming force against us in the vicinity of Tupelo, and the utter hopelessness of saving our train or artillery in case of defeat, on account of the narrowness and general bad condition of the roads and the impossibility of procuring supplies of forage for the animals." Sturgis had a point. The expedition had reached a crossroads that would determine its destiny. Sturgis recalled that all at the meeting "agreed with me in the probable consequences of defeat."[66]

While all may have agreed with the probable consequences of defeat, not everyone had the same opinion. Those in attendance other than Sturgis included General Grierson, Colonel McMillen, Colonel Hoge and Captain S.L. Woodward. Grierson explained his view of the situation as he knew it, believing that "to make a further advance would be hazardous. If the general felt that he must go forward, rations and other supplies should be issued to the command and the supply train left there or sent back." Grierson found the wagon train to be an encumbrance but realized that the troops would need to return to Memphis at some point soon because "our supplies were being rapidly exhausted." Sturgis then called upon McMillen, who also agreed that an advance would be hazardous yet, according to Grierson, spoke in an "excited and rather contemptuous manner of the idea of turning back." Unlike Grierson, who had missed Sturgis's first expedition from Memphis back in May due to illness, McMillen had been part of the expedition and remembered the difficulties. He recalled how the expedition had returned without achieving satisfactory results. He had been in favor of the first expedition's return, but this time was a different matter. McMillen was in favor of moving forward, so much so that Grierson recalled McMillen to state that he would continue the march "with the whole outfit, transportation and all, until the enemy was found and attacked." He further added, "If we went back without a fight, we would be disgraced," and said that he would rather "go on and be whipped than to return to Ripley." Grierson, not wanting to have the appearance of backing down from a fight, reiterated his view but also added that if the decision was to continue to move forward, "I should go on and fight the foe wherever found." He added, "My best judgment still led me to believe that if General Sturgis advanced his column beyond Ripley, through mud and rain, encumbered by transportation and camp equipage, it would result in disaster to our troops, and that the colonel would be apt to have all the fighting he desired before he got back to Memphis."[67]

The loneliness of command surely fell on Sturgis this day. To turn back now would be seen as certain defeat by the authorities in Memphis and beyond. Sturgis remembered how he had already called off the first expedition due to the "utter and entire destitution of the country," and now he would end a second expedition based mainly on the same excuse. This would not work. He would have to at least meet the enemy first before thinking of going back to Memphis. Sturgis reasoned that Washburn had received information that "there could be no considerable force in our front and all my own information led to the same conclusion." Sturgis realized, "My information was exceedingly meager and unsatisfactory, and had I returned I would have been totally unable to present any facts to justify my course, or show why the expedition might not have been successfully carried forward." To continue forward could bring ultimate ruin or possible victory. It was a difficult situation to be in. However, the decision was made. Sturgis and his men would move forward. Outside, the rain continued to fall in torrents.[68]

It was June 7 when Forrest received word that the Union expedition was moving toward the area of Ruckersville. Now that he knew Sturgis was in Ripley, Forrest still could not know which roads Sturgis would yet take. Now was the time for Confederate forces to pull together what they could and gravitate toward Forrest and north Mississippi. The weather that plagued Sturgis did not let up for Forrest and his men either. As Buford marched his men toward Booneville, he soon found that the rains had significantly swollen Twenty-mile Creek. It was quickly found that the creek could not be forded. This didn't bode well for the artillery and wagons. Also, once past this creek, Wolf Creek lay only two miles farther on, and it also needed to be bridged. Details were called on to build the bridges, and the first was completed and the men moved forward. However, according to R.R. Hancock of the 2nd Tennessee Cavalry, "The water by this time was out in Wolf Creek bottom so that it would be over axle deep to wagons before reaching the bridge…besides it was now growing late in the afternoon." This didn't stop Buford. About three hundred yards from Wolf Creek, the command halted. Buford went to the creek and sent back for his staff officers to join him. "To their great surprise and chagrin," according to Hancock, Buford thundered out, "'Dismount, I want you to help build this bridge—I want to see you get wet.' It was really amusing to us to see how completely they were taken down as Buford would take them by the arm with one hand while he pointed out what he wanted them to do with the other. And it had the desired effect, too, for we did not mind what we had to do after he put those officers to work." Hancock added, "After the bridge was completed we decided that we had seen fun enough to pay us very well for all we had done." Needless to say, Buford and the whole division, along with its wagons and artillery, were north of Wolf Creek before sundown.[69]

Forrest and Buford's division moved out to Baldwyn and, by the morning of June 8, toward Booneville. Lee was also attentive to the Union march and ordered Colonel Rucker, commanding Kentuckians of the Sixth Brigade of Forrest's command, to move out and assist Forrest. All was busy on June 8, but not everything was of a positive nature. Within the Confederate line was a boxcar in which could be found three deserters. Morton recalled that "a preacher was with them, and I can still hear their voices in prayer and singing hymns." The three were to be shot the next day. "The next morning the clouds had passed away and the woods were jubilant with the twittering of birds." However, this did not stop military obligations. Three newly dug graves could be found near a field where a command of soldiers had been secured, along with the three blindfolded deserters. Morton continued, "A sharp command, a crack of musketry, and two lives are snuffed out like worthless tallow candles. One of them was spared on account of his extreme youth. Will he ever forget the moment he knelt by that open grave and heard that crack of musketry?" By the evening of June 9, Rucker and his men had joined Forrest at Booneville.[70]

Forrest now had his forces spread out across northeast Mississippi. This could make for better communications as they watched the Union army's movement; however, once Sturgis's plans were developed, getting all of the Confederate forces together to give battle was another issue. On the evening of June 9, Forrest called a meeting of those of his command who were near him, that being Generals Buford and Rucker and Chief of Artillery Morton. Forrest had been receiving word that Union forces were concentrated and encamped only twelve miles east of the town of Ripley on what was known as the Ripley-Guntown road. Sturgis's plan of using the more northern route was abandoned as impracticable due to rains and muddy roads. Forrest now had a direction and road the Union expedition would be traveling down, and he didn't waste time. The place the Union forces had camped was also known as Stubb's farm. This farm was only about nine miles from Brice's Crossroads. It was at these crossroads that the Ripley and Guntown road crossed the road from Baldwyn to Pontotoc. At these crossroads, the Union army could fall upon Baldwyn only five miles away or take the Guntown road six miles into Guntown. The Mobile & Ohio Railroad ran through Baldwyn and Guntown, making both towns more vital to each side's cause.[71]

Forrest made plans for June 10, but when they were developed, they were not without their fair share of controversy. General Stephen D. Lee would write much later in 1902 that the plan was not to fight at Brice's Crossroads. It was after Forrest received word that Sturgis was moving on the Ripley-Guntown road the night of June 9 that Forrest issued orders to move his men quickly to the south in order to get in front of Sturgis's expedition. Forrest's plan was to "reach and pass Brice's Crossroads before the Federal army reached that point." Furthermore, Lee recounted, "Gen. Lee and Gen. Forrest were together in consultation at Baldwin when a change of plans by the enemy was first known. It was decided that Forrest should throw his command rapidly in front of Gen. Sturgis, and if possible, draw him farther towards Okolona before fighting." In doing so, Lee would have more time to collect Confederate forces before doing battle with a foe that was believed to be twice that of Forrest's command. Forrest believed he could get in front of Sturgis before that general reached the crossroads. Captain Sam Donaldson, an aide of Forrest, later wrote, "The next day much to the surprise of Gen. Forrest, the commands of Grierson and Sturgis appeared in force, and the great Battle of Tishomingo Creek was fought that afternoon." Therefore, Lee had left his meeting with Forrest believing that the real battle would not be fought at Brice's Crossroads but near Okolona. At 10:00 a.m., Forrest sent a telegraph to Lee at Okolona stating, "Enemy are advancing directly on this place; Johnson's brigade is here; Buford's division and Rucker's brigade with two batteries will be here by 12 o'clock; our pickets have already commenced firing. N.B. Forrest, Major General." It was at this point, with the enemy in his path, that Forrest decided to give battle with what troops he had.[72]

Others believed that Forrest had planned to fight Sturgis at Brice's Crossroads and not at Okolona, as Lee expected. Lee, in a correspondence of 1897, admitted that "Forrest had not been ordered to avoid a conflict with Sturgis under any and all circumstances. While he believed that Sturgis could ultimately be defeated, and that the defeat, taking place farther down in Mississippi, would prove more disastrous to the Federal expedition, he left General Forrest with full discretion to act in any emergency as his judgment might dictate."[73]

It was Colonel Rucker who would add to the controversy concerning the evening meeting of June 9 when Forrest explained to his officers that while he would like to get the enemy in the open country as Lee had communicated, he also believed that a situation might "arise which would necessitate a conflict before the prairie country could be reached, and before a concentration with General Lee and Chalmers in the vicinity of Okolona could be effected." For Forrest, it appeared that a fight would prove almost inevitable, and Brice's Crossroads would most likely be the place. While riding with Forrest on the morning of June 10, Rucker chanced an interesting discourse with Forrest. While Forrest and Rucker rode next to each other ahead of the Confederate column, Forrest explained, "I know they greatly outnumber the troops I have at hand, but the road along which they will march is narrow and muddy; they will make slow progress. The country is densely wooded and the undergrowth so heavy that when we strike them they will not know how few men we have. Their cavalry will move out ahead of the infantry, and should reach the cross-roads three hours in advance." He further stated, "We can whip their cavalry in that time. As soon as the fight opens they will send back to have the infantry hurried up. It is going to be as hot as hell, and coming on a run for five or six miles over such roads, their infantry will be so tired out we will ride right over them. I want everything to move up as fast as possible. I will go ahead with Lyon and the escort and open the fight."[74]

Regardless of the various communications and perceptions as to locales of battle, Brice's Crossroads would be a most advantageous landmark for Forrest to take and hold—if he could get there first. Forrest issued orders for his men to be on the move at 4:00 a.m. on the morning of June 10. Before dawn approached, Forrest's men rode out toward Pontotoc by moving through Baldwyn.[75] The race was on.

On the morning of June 9, while at Stubb's farm, Sturgis found it necessary to free his army of as many encumbrances as possible. Therefore, he sent back to Memphis "as many wagons, sick soldiers, and disabled horses as possible, and to issue five days' rations to the command, we left camp," Sturgis recalled, "a little late, sending back to Memphis 400 sick, 41 wagons, and a large number of worn-out horses."[76]

While at Stubb's farm, Grierson, Captain Woodward and Lieutenants Pike and McClure tried to buoy their spirits and went into the house. That night they found an old piano, a worn-out violin consisting of three strings and a bow in about the same condition. The young lady who lived there wanted music to sing by, and the officers joined in. Grierson remembered how the lady had, "a voice as tuneless and twanging as the instrument, but much more powerful…emphasizing and prolonging the words, spitting between the lines, and looked languishingly over her shoulder for our approval and admiration." Grierson took the "old cracked fiddle, while the company joined hands in a merry dance." While the group enjoyed the evening, Grierson pondered, "It is well to make the most of life as it comes to us, and to be merry even under the most unfavorable circumstances."[77] On this night, Grierson would fiddle, while tomorrow the Union wagons would burn.

Chapter 3

"The Critical Hour of the Battle"

June 10 was a new day for Sturgis and the expedition. The rains that had fallen so heavily had finally ceased. Captain James C. Foster found the morning "dawned clear and exceedingly hot, even for that climate." Sturgis and McMillen were awake and had a drink of whiskey just before breakfast. At this time, Grierson stopped by, once again, to voice his concerns of masses of Rebels not far away waiting to attack as the expedition moved forward. He went on to request that the wagons and infantry stay at Stubb's farm due to the fact that the "mules of the train were exhausted and in bad condition after their great exertion in pulling the heavy loaded wagons through the deep mud in which they were frequently mired." Grierson went further in advising the general that Stubb's farm was a good position to fight from in case the enemy did attack. At least the ground would be of their choosing and the cavalry would be able to move out and more accurately understand the Confederate troop strength, thus drawing them forward into an engagement. Sturgis, believing there were no Confederate troops of significant size to his front, continued the expedition's advance. Furthermore, Grierson was ordered to take his division and "to keep it well in advance of, and out of the way of the infantry and train." Grierson was to march on Baldwyn.[78]

Sturgis reassured Grierson that he should attack the enemy wherever he might find them and that once involved, the infantry, who would be "well closed up," would move on to Guntown. Grierson was to attack the enemy on site and push them back. For Sturgis, the numbers just were not there to think Grierson would face a powerful enemy, at least not until possibly near Okolona. Sturgis had expected the Federal cavalry to be up and marching at 5:30 a.m. on the morning of June 10, with the infantry to follow around 7:00 a.m. The order of march included the cavalry in front, followed by the artillery and then infantry with its artillery and finally the supply train guarded by the rear brigade. One of the Third Brigade regiments was at the head of the wagons, one near the middle and one following in the rear with a section of artillery for protection. Pioneers were sent out ahead of the infantry in order to repair roads, build bridges or take care of any other impediments that might turn up. As it were, the pioneers, if not the complete expedition other than the cavalry, would find severe problems just five miles out of camp.[79]

Sturgis rode to the front of the infantry as they made their way along the Guntown road and right into what he called "an unusually bad place in the road, and one that would require considerable time and labor to render practicable." What Sturgis found was Hatchie Bottom. Colonel D.C. Thomas remembered the bottom quite well: "It was a quarter of a mile over the worst part of the road; seventy or eighty rods." Thomas added, "It appeared to be a sort of a quicksand, with soft places where the mud was deeper and softer than in others." It was here, as Sturgis was waiting for the head of the column, that he received a message from Grierson stating that he had at least a portion of the Confederate cavalry in his front.[80] More messages quickly followed.

Colonel Tyree H. Bell's Confederate brigade had left Rienzi by daylight except for Newson's regiment, which was in the Corinth area. Later that morning, Bell entered Booneville, and while issuing rations, he learned that Forrest had left before daylight in order to get the march on Sturgis. Buford was also in Booneville, and now Buford and Bell with his brigade moved toward Brice's Crossroads. Hancock of the 7th Tennessee Cavalry took note of the day: "The night had been rainy, but the sun rose brightly, and dispelling the morning mist, became warm and somewhat oppressive to the men and jaded horses; and the roads, saturated with water from recent continuous heavy rains, were so much cut up as to retard the progress of the artillery."[81] Forrest moved forward on the Baldwyn road toward Brice's Crossroads with Lyon's brigade and Rucker's brigade to follow. While some of Forrest's brigades were spread out, they were within striking distance of Brice's Crossroads. Forrest was gambling on the idea that if and when the fight occurred, he would be able to rely on these brigades to follow through. It was a question of timing. Bell's and Johnson's brigades were within the area, but it would take time to bring them toward the battle. Of the Confederate soldiers within the ranks for the day's battle, Rucker had 700 men and Johnson had a mere 500, while Lyon had 800. Lyon's brigade was not far away at Baldwyn. Bell had almost 2,800 men, which was more than half of Forrest's available troops for this fight. However, Forrest would later report that his available force during this fight stood at only 3,500.[82] Captain F.C. Terry, who was serving on Buford's staff at the moment, recalled, "At daylight Lyon, with the Kentucky brigade of Buford's division was ordered to take the road to Tupelo and find the enemy and engage him." Buford, along with Morton's and Rice's batteries, was to remain at Booneville, and once Bell had joined him, the column would follow after Lyon. Bell's forces met Buford's around 7:30 a.m.[83]

Forrest and his men were moving toward the crossroads as quickly as possible, yet after receiving intelligence from persons in Old Carrollville, Forrest soon learned that the Union cavalry was only about four miles from the crossroads. In order to slow down the enemy movement, Forrest sent forward Lieutenant Black of his staff with men of the 7th Tennessee Cavalry to ascertain the situation. Not long after, Forrest received word that Black had met the advance of the Union cavalry about one and a half miles north of the crossroads and was skirmishing with the Union forces at that time. No doubt these were the Union forces of Captain Robert N. Hanson's patrol, which included the 4th Missouri Cavalry on the Baldwyn road.[84] Forrest quickly ordered his lead troops, Lyon and his Kentuckians, to "move forward and develop the enemy." From here, Forrest fired off to Buford a message to move up with the artillery along with Bell's command to move as rapidly as possible, at least as fast as the muddy roads and worn-out horses could permit. In a strategic move, Forrest also called for Buford to send forward a regiment from Bell's brigade moving from Old Carrollville and across to the Ripley-Guntown road, thereby gaining the rear of the Union forces, or least to "attack and annoy his rear or flank."[85]

Bell was moving his men forward with great haste as the artillery continued to try to keep up with them. Bell remembered that morning, "The artillery had great difficulty in passing over the muddy roads, swollen streams and on one occasion before reaching the battle ground, a gun broke through a bridge but was soon hauled out and the bridge repaired and the artillery moved on in the direction of Brice's Crossroads, and firing could be distinctly heard from the front."[86]

About a mile and a half out on the Baldwyn road and moving west toward the crossroads, Lyon had Captain Randle and his dismounted

The area to the left of the Baldwyn road looking south, where Forrest gathered his men for the beginning of the attack against the Union cavalry. This is east of Brice's Crossroads. *Courtesy of Emilee Bennett.*

company of troopers move forward in order to feel out the Union line. It wasn't long before these men found the enemy, which was just in the distance and considered "strongly posted in heavy force in front."[87] Companies A and C of the 12th Kentucky Cavalry, under the command of Captain Tyler, were now called forward. After reporting to the front, Tyler recalled meeting with Forrest and Lyon, whereupon the Union line was to the front and in view of all to see. Forrest, while pointing to the Federal troops up ahead, directed Tyler to "charge them and see how many were there." At the gallop, Tyler and his cavalry moved forward and quickly received a warm reception of leaden hail from Warring's brigade, which was in line of battle. Tyler recalled, "I withdrew perhaps a little faster than I advanced."[88]

Due to these developments, Forrest had the rest of Lyon's Kentuckians dismounted and formed for battle. This included the 3rd Kentucky and 12th Kentucky Cavalry Regiments. The 3rd Kentucky dismounted and moved forward on the double-quick to help support Randle and his men. The regiment found itself immediately in the day's action. The Kentucky brigade covered both sides of the Baldwyn road, with the 7th Kentucky to the right of the road. The 7th Kentucky struggled in its movement forward as the blackjack, scrub oak and undergrowth in general grew thick and caused many to not be able to see more than fifty yards in front of them. Fortunately, fighting dismounted was not a difficult task for any of the Kentucky boys.

The 3rd, 7th and 8th had for almost three years served as infantry regiments before being assigned to Forrest's command. Henry Hord of the 3rd Kentucky was one of the infantry-turned-cavalry and believed these Kentuckians "had all an infantryman's contempt for cavalry fighting; but they changed their opinion before they had been with old Bedford long."[89]

These troops managed to push back the Union defenders toward the edge of an old field about three hundred yards closer to the crossroads. The 7th and 12th Kentucky now advanced, with the 7th on the right of the line and the 12th to the left. Two companies of the 12th, however, were held back in order to guard the flanks while Kentuckians of the 8th Regiment were held in reserve and at the center of the line. Supposedly, during this first encounter with Union troops, there was a cotton gin situated about one hundred yards off to the right of the Baldwyn road with a small field that extended east along the road. It was here that some of the Kentuckians charged the Union soldiers who had taken a position just behind the gin.[90]

Samuel A. Agnew was awake early on June 10, like most citizens around the Brice's Crossroads community. He was settled into a morning breakfast in his white two-story home on a ridge about two miles northwest of Brice's Crossroads. While eating with his father and brother, news came that the "Yankees had camped the night before at Stubb's farm, seven miles from us in the direction of Ripley." Samuel moved quickly and took his father's mules and horses, "with some Negroes to help care for them and a little brother then thirteen years old, went into a dense thicket a mile and a half southwest of our home, where we hoped to hide our stock and save them from seizure by Federal troops if they came our way." The boys stayed in the bottom of a branch behind the farm. Agnew recalled, "We heard a roaring northward which we could not explain. Afterward we knew it was the noise made by the advancing Federal army." They were unable to communicate with their family back at home. All they could do was listen and anxiously wait to see what might occur. It wasn't long until "a volley of small arms was heard—it was the first shots of the day." Unknown to Agnew at the time, when the battle started, his mother, wife and sisters "closed the window shutters, all went into an inner room and, lying flat on the floor, they awaited the issue of the conflict…The yard was a battle ground." Little did the Agnews know that their home would become part of the last stand in the battle of Brice's Crossroads.[91]

While the community was starting to realize what was happening in their own front yards, the Kentuckians moved forward enough to take the ridge the Federals had been driven from. At this point, Lyon found that Union troops were being massed in his front, leading him to believe that the enemy might be planning an attack at any time. Lyon had his men throw together fortifications, which included fence rails, logs, fallen timber and anything else that could help stop a Yankee bullet.[92]

The addition of Rucker's brigade of 700, coupled with 500 men from Johnson's brigade, gave Forrest an additional 1,200 troops that he sorely needed. What was still missing, however, was General Buford, Bell's brigade and Morton's artillery. It was only a question of time as to when these troops would arrive. Until that time, Forrest continued what he recalled as a "severe skirmish with the enemy, which was kept up until 1 o'clock." How long Grierson would take to finally turn Forrest's shortened

Reverend Samuel A. Agnew. *Courtesy of Sam Agnew, Private Collection.*

flanks and possibly rout his inferior numbers was unclear. For the moment, however, the skirmish line held and the firing continued.[93]

A skirmisher faced various dangerous situations when on the front line looking for the enemy. He could usually expect to be the hunter as well as the hunted. One such case was evident early in the fighting. A company of thirty to forty men of the 8th Kentucky Mounted Infantry created a skirmish line to the regiment's front. These men were ordered forward with the brigade, following about one hundred yards behind them. The skirmish line was not the safest place to be that morning. W.D. Brown of these skirmishers remembered, "We had not gone far when the sharp crack of Enfields indicated that the conflict was on." The skirmishers were spread out from fifteen to twenty feet apart. Brown found himself in the timber and to the left of the Baldwyn road. "I could see the Yankee skirmishers dodging from one tree to another for shelter. I went through a yard by a little log house to my left, and crossed the fence into the woods." Brown continued, "A Yankee crept up obliquely to my right just across the public road, taking advantage of a stump for shelter, and as he put his gun over the stump…Capt. Jones saw him and hallooed to me, 'Look out!'

at the same time firing his pistol at Mr. Yankee, who quickly took shelter behind a friendly tree just in time to save his scalp."[94]

Sturgis's command was not the only one dealing with the elements and logistics this day. Morton was doing all he could to follow orders and move his artillery or, as some called them, Morton's Bull Pups to the front as quickly as possible. Horses were "jaded" from their long march from Russellville and back, and now it was "almost impossible for them to drag the guns over the eighteen intervening miles of unusually deep mud." The cavalry horses did little better. Morton's guns continued to fall farther behind, only to receive order after order to hurry forward. Bell watched as "every thing was cleared from the road and the artillery moved at all possible speed until reaching within a mile of the Cross Roads." The horses moved to a gallop until "the last few miles were made in a frantic run, and the two batteries crossed the creek 'bottom' and passed up a rise which brought them to…'the critical hour of the battle.'"[95]

While Forrest would be coming toward Brice's Crossroads from the east through the scrub oak and blackjack, Union forces would be coming from the west through the cornfields, across the creek and then to the Brice's Crossroads intersection. Before Grierson and his men arrived, Brice's Crossroads had been a quiet place. There was a small country store, a few outbuildings and the Brice house, which had not been completed for long before Sturgis's men paid their visit. The Brice home was "a two story twelve room house with porticos in front." It was considered by some to be "after the fashion of the latest southern mansion," and it stood for some time after the war. Altogether, it was believed that only about forty or fifty acres of the land was cleared. In all directions around the crossroads could be found heavy timber, along with thick undergrowth of blackjack and scrub oak with bushes mixed with vines and briers. If and when troops moved off the road and into the fields, woods and thickets, they could expect to move slowly. This was especially true for horses and artillery. It was also believed that troops could still move through the morass of woods and undergrowth, but again, very slowly. Looking south of the Guntown road and east of the Pontotoc road, the environment was similar, with some open wooded areas and large trees. To the right of the Guntown road about four hundred yards east from Brice's Crossroads was a large cotton field. However, north of the Guntown road parallel with the road and about five hundred yards away could be found a wooded ravine through which a stream ran west to the Tishomingo Creek.[96]

Morton's Artillery, from *Life of Lieutenant-General Nathan Bedford Forrest* by John Allan Wyeth. *Author's collection.*

Just about half a mile northwest of Brice's Crossroads, Tishomingo Creek could be found. The banks of the Tishomingo were considered high and very soft, especially since the heavy rains had filled it close to its banks. This made it difficult for horses or men to cross without using the bridge. The Tishomingo Creek ran lazily from north to south and back behind the crossroads. However, it could rage with great force during heavy rains, such as those encountered around June 10. The bridge itself was old, narrow

Tishomingo Creek today. *Courtesy of Emilee Bennett.*

and the only bridge for several miles. The strategic positive and negative to the situation around Brice's Crossroads was that it was easy to move upon the enemy within yards of their position without being detected. However, the enemy could do the same. Throughout the area, the grounds were undulating without breaking into sharp ridges. Interestingly, the area behind the crossroads to the northwest toward the creek steadily dropped about one hundred feet. From the east, the Ripley-Guntown road descended from the high banks of the crossroads to a bottom flat area near Tishomingo Creek. Across this creek was the bridge, with cornfields on either side of the creek. Just north of the Ripley-Guntown road, near the creek and across from the field south of the same road, was a ridge about fifty feet high and several hundred feet long with woods and a cabin. The west side of this ridge ended about seventy feet from Tishomingo Creek. The ridge continued east about one hundred feet and then shifted to the northeast for about two hundred yards. The Ripley-Guntown road ran along the south edge of this ridge and then bore to the right and up toward Brice's Crossroads. It was about a half mile from the creek to the crossroads and Brice's house.[97]

Grierson recalled that it was about 10:00 a.m. when his forces reached Brice's Crossroads. At this point, patrols were sent out over the roads that

Log Cabin Ridge looking north from the field where part of Sturgis's wagon train was parked. The Ripley-Guntown road is situated between the two. *Author's collection.*

included Baldwyn, Guntown and Pontotoc. Waring's brigade was brought forward, made to dismount at the crossroads and told to wait for further developments. Captain Robert N. Hanson's patrol, which included the 4th Missouri Cavalry, had moved no more than about a mile and a half east on the Baldwyn road when his troops were fired upon by what seemed to be a strong picket of the enemy, most likely Lyon's Kentuckians. Grierson, along with Waring, took the 9th and 3rd Illinois Cavalry and 2nd New Jersey Cavalry, along with a section of howitzers, to reinforce Hanson. Waring then ordered a staff officer to take the remainder of the brigade and form it into a line of battle along the edge of a thicket just a half mile east of Brice's Crossroads and facing an open field. By advancing, Waring was able to get a better view of the lay of the land but not much more. In no time, Confederates were again firing into them, forcing the Federals back to their line of battle.[98]

Waring developed his battle line as the following: On the Baldwyn road were placed the four mountain howitzers belonging to the 4th Missouri Cavalry, including the regiment to the left in line. On their left was a squadron of the 7th Indiana Cavalry. To the right of the battery could be found two battalions of the 7th Indiana Cavalry, with the rest of the regiment held in reserve. The 2nd New Jersey Cavalry was also in reserve and ready to reinforce the right wing if called upon to do so. The 9th and 3rd Illinois Cavalry were placed to the front of the battery on lower ground and served as skirmishers, taking shelter behind trees and logs. Due to the nature of the topography, all of these cavalrymen were dismounted.[99]

Forrest was skirmishing for time at this point in the fight. It would have been to the general's advantage if he and his men had taken and controlled Brice's Crossroads before Grierson, but that was not the case. Now Forrest needed to buy time until the rest of his troops could get on the battlefield. What was important now was to keep Grierson at bay while also keeping the initiative. Lyon's brigade of only eight hundred rank and file troops would be hard pressed if Grierson and the Union cavalry decided to take offensive measures. Bell's men, along with Morton's artillery, were still some miles away, and Rucker's and Johnson's were close. Forrest needed to keep Grierson off balance while not bringing on a full-scale battle since most of Forrest's troops were still absent from the field. In a quick decision, Forrest opted for the offensive, thereby keeping the initiative. Acting on the offensive aggressively seemed to be in Forrest's blood. In the past, he had a discussion with a Union officer in which Forrest explained that he would "give more for fifteen minutes of bulge on the enemy than for a week of tactics." In other words, timing and getting more troops to the fight first, or getting the "bulge" on the enemy, played a crucial factor in winning the battle. The more time a commander had, the better chance of getting more troops onto the field of his choosing. Also, Forrest was not known for standing to receive an attack. Instead, he followed the idea that "one man in motion was worth two standing to receive an attack."[100]

To Forrest's great relief, Rucker's brigade arrived on the battlefield and was sent to the left of the Kentucky brigade. Rucker's men had been in the saddle for seven hours and had traveled eighteen miles. Now they had to be ready for a day's hard fighting. Rucker's men of the 18th Mississippi Cavalry and 7th Tennessee Cavalry were dismounted, but the 8th Mississippi Cavalry, also known as Duff's Mississippians, continued to stay mounted and moved out toward the extreme left of the Confederate line. This was needed in order to combat any Union forces that might try to perform a flanking movement in that sector. It wasn't long before Rucker's men found themselves "warmly engaged" with Grierson's forces, which were protecting themselves behind "a fence and dense thicket of dwarf-oaks." As the firing continued, Forrest also greeted the arrival of Colonel Johnson and his

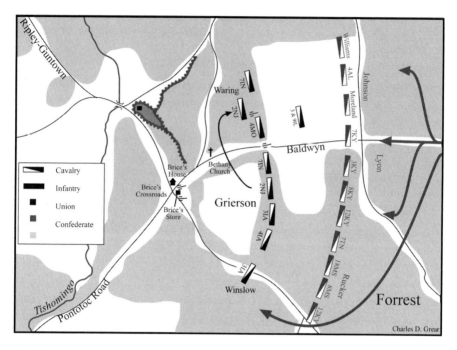

Confederate attack against Grierson's cavalry. *Courtesy of Dr. Charles Grear.*

brigade of Alabamians. These men moved to the right of Lyon's Kentucky troops and on the Confederate right of the Baldwyn road.[101]

Now, Forrest would put his belief in keeping the initiative to action. He ordered Lyon to once again take the initiative and move forward. Johnston would also move forward on the far Confederate right, with Rucker moving on the Confederate left. While Forrest saw this as a "severe skirmish," it was anything but that for Johnson's Alabamians and Lyon's Kentuckians as they made their way through the tangled mess they found before them on the right of the Baldwyn road. Those to the left of the road moved through the mix of woods and fields.[102]

As the Kentuckians had moved forward in their first attack earlier in the day, they found that in the field and woods before them were the 7th Indiana Cavalry. These Indianans formed their battle line on a hill to the right of the Baldwyn road behind a rail fence. The skirmish line was "advanced to near the middle of the marsh in front of the line." However, the marsh in question was mostly, if not completely, created by the many days of rainfall that had saturated the lands around Brice's Crossroads. From their position, the boys from Indiana could see the Confederate line just to the front on the next hill. For the enemy to advance, one Indianan recalled, "they would be obliged to cross the open swamp between the two lines, and be exposed to the fire from the Federal lines concealed in the woods."[103]

Union skirmishers were sent out, and with the battery of the 4th Missouri Cavalry to the 7th Indiana's immediate left, a "very lively fire" was kept up. Lieutenant Colonel Thomas M. Browne of the Indiana regiment received an order from Waring in no uncertain terms to "hold the position occupied by us to the last extremity." Therefore, the men lay on the ground close to the fence, reserving their fire until the Confederates were in close range. At this point, the Kentuckians continued a brisk skirmish fire at long range. The time for an attack would come soon enough.[104]

The skirmish lines came to life with heavy fire as the Confederates attacked along the lines of Lyon and Johnson. From the Confederate line came a "loud cheer," and according to Thomas S. Cogley of the 7th Indiana Cavalry, "almost immediately massed columns emerged from the woods occupied by the rebels, and began crossing the open space." The Union line held its fire as the Confederates moved closer. Finally, the Union line released a dreadful fire into the oncoming line, causing them to fall back in confusion, thus retreating back up the hill. This didn't stop a second attack as the gray line moved forward once again. This time, they met the same fate as Union guns spewed forth death on the hapless troops. Now, the Kentuckians formed in the field and fired a volley on the 7th Indianans but with little effect, if any. Not only were the soldiers of Lyon's brigade taking well-directed fire from the men in their front, but the 14th Indiana and 4th Missouri artillery batteries were raking the Confederates as well. Colonel Thomas M. Browne spoke of these batteries and recalled, "I passed up to the batteries and watched with delight the effect of the bursting bombs. They made the rebels scatter delightfully."[105]

Again, Lyon's men advanced toward the blue line. Around this time, Captain Moore of Company H, 7th Indiana Cavalry, was ordered by Colonel Waring to take his men to the far left of the line as reinforcements. Apparently, Johnson and his men were making themselves known in the deep thicket they were engaged in. These men had been dismounted and directed to attract the attention of the far left Union line. The most that could be said of their fighting was that it included about five minutes of "desultory fire" before they retired, and Major Hanson would write of the incident that "a small force, less than three hundred, moved against the extreme left of Waring's brigade, but was easily repulsed." Regardless of the fire or lack of fire from Johnson's line, it did serve its purpose in attracting the attention of the Union army, thus causing Company H of the 7th Indiana Cavalry to move to the support of the far left and weakening the 7th Indiana's main line.[106]

The loss of Company H left roughly 280 men to hold the 7th Indiana's position. It was actually fewer than that, as 1 in every 4 men was assigned behind the line as a horse holder. The men were in single rank along the line. This time, when the gray line flowed across the field, the troops met in close quarters. Before this occurred, however, not long after Company H was reassigned, another request came requiring the 2nd New Jersey Cavalry to move from its position and protect Waring's left, north of the Baldwyn road. Colonel Browne had no other choice but to thin out his line and connect with the 3rd Iowa of Winslow's Second Brigade. This caused the 7th Indiana Cavalry to become Waring's far right regiment.[107] It only got worse for Browne and the 7th Indiana Cavalry as they watched Rucker's men also coming toward them from the east and southeast.

Lyon's and Rucker's troopers were relentless as the Indianans tried desperately to push them back and hold the line. First Lieutenant Cogley of the 7th Indiana Cavalry remembered the anguish of the day: "The muzzle of carbine or musket was placed against the body of the assailants or the assailed, and discharged. In many instances, the men not having time to re-load their carbines, used them as clubs over the heads of the rebels, and even clinched and pounded them with their fists." Cogley further recalled, "The rebels on getting over the fence were either shot, and fell on either side of it, or were knocked off either with the butts of the carbines, or with the fist." As the fight continued, the men of the 7th Indiana found that they could not withstand the punishment of the Confederate assault. Browne and the men of the 7th Indiana were desperate. Browne dispatched one of his orderlies to Waring, asking for reinforcements to be sent to the 7th Indiana's right flank. The request fell on deaf ears. Waring made it clear that "he had already disposed of every available man in the brigade, and that to give me assistance was impossible." It was too late. Confederate forces were now attempting to turn the 7th Indiana's right. Finally, the Confederates carried the fence line, but the fight continued "from bush to bush and from tree to tree." Browne's right had been broken.[108]

Within this retrograde movement, some men of the 7th Indiana Cavalry could find solace in the fact that they found good use for their navy revolvers. As the Kentuckians continued their surge forward at close range, "Many a rebel in feeling his way through the heavy foliage of the bushes, found the muzzle of a navy in his face and bid good-bye to the world." The hand-to-

Hand to Hand, from *Life of Lieutenant-General Nathan Bedford Forrest* by John Allan Wyeth. *Author's collection.*

hand fighting and navy revolvers served to slow the Confederate tide rising across the field.[109] However, the right of the 7th Indiana Cavalry was having its own troubles with Lyon's troops and those of Rucker. Parts of Waring's line had seen heavy fighting and would have been flanked if it had not been for the men of Winslow's brigade coming upon the crossroads and continuing the Union line out toward the Guntown road. As Lyon and

Johnson's men attacked or were in a "heavy skirmish," Rucker's men had also moved across the field.

Waring's four howitzers could be heard along the Union line that now formed around the crossroads. Men of the 3rd and 12th Kentucky moved forward through the field in a forced reconnaissance and found what cover they could. This skirmish helped keep Grierson off balance and his soldiers on the defensive. In doing so, Grierson played right into Forrest's hands. Instead of attacking what one Union officer would later describe as a "line of the enemy…somewhat shorter than that of the cavalry in position," Grierson sent messages back to Sturgis, adamantly stating in one that the Confederate forces to his front must be between six and seven thousand men.[110] There was no way that Grierson was going to take a chance and attack Forrest's troops and pass on toward Baldwyn. Forrest's bluff of an all-out attack had paid off, and he had bought the time he desperately needed.

After about an hour of heavy skirmishing, reinforcements began to arrive, and the Kentuckians moved back to their line of makeshift breastworks. This could have been an excellent opportunity for Grierson and his commanders to defeat Forrest. Major Hanson of the 4th Missouri Cavalry recalled the Confederate advance stating, "They advanced until the right of their line came under the rapid and flanking fire at short range of the skirmishers with revolving rifles, when it wavered and halted, and with but little disorder the entire force fell back to the wood." What disturbed Hanson was the fact that "no effort was made to follow and turn the retreat into rout, and none to throw troops upon either flank, the right flank being vulnerable from Waring's brigade and the left from Winslow's." The most that happened at this time was that a skirmish fire was continued at long range.[111]

Earlier in the day, when skirmishing had first broken out and was heard from the east of the crossroads between Forrest's and Waring's men, Colonel Winslow's men of the Second Brigade could be found working on the bridge at Tishomingo Creek. The bridge was in such bad shape that, according to Grierson, Winslow "had halted his command and caused it [the bridge] to be thoroughly reconstructed, which proved to be a thoughtful precaution, subsequently of much importance to the command."[112] There wasn't much to this old bridge. Private James H. White of the 3rd Iowa Cavalry, Company H, remembered the bridge as merely "a pole bridge about 10 ft wide." Winslow had been hearing the guns of Waring's command since 11:00 a.m. It was not until 12:00 p.m., however, that he and his command were finally ordered by Grierson to move to the right of Waring's brigade, where Winslow's cavalrymen were to defend the Guntown and Pontotoc roads. Grierson, believing it to be "entirely impracticable" to try to force his way to Baldwyn and remembering that Sturgis had directed him to fight Forrest wherever he could find him, decided to "obstruct his advance and to hold the position" at least until reinforced by the infantry. Besides, Grierson believed that Sturgis was close by. By 12:30 p.m., the 3rd Iowa Cavalry was sent forward and to the right of the 2nd New Jersey Cavalry, along with eight companies of the 4th Iowa to the right of the 3rd Iowa Cavalry. These troops were also dismounted and put into line about a half mile from Brice's Crossroads. Now that the left of the Second Brigade had joined the right of the First Brigade, the Union line formed a quarter to half circle encompassing the Baldwyn and Guntown roads. The deployment of skirmishers was positioned a good distance in front of Winslow's brigade. On the extreme right toward the Pontotoc road could be found the 10th Missouri Cavalry and 7th Illinois Cavalry. Together, these two regiments totaled two hundred men. Winslow also sent back to the rear four companies belonging to the 4th Iowa Cavalry in order to keep in communication with the train and protect it. Winslow now made his way over to his troops along the Union line protecting the Guntown road.[113]

Captain H.S. Lee of the 7th Wisconsin Battery was not only in charge of the two pieces of artillery from Wisconsin, but he also oversaw the artillery of the Cavalry Division if and when an engagement was to occur during the expedition. That time was now. For added protection of the roads, the two-gun battery of the 10th Missouri, Company A, helped to command the crossroads. His command now consisted of his two artillery pieces, two pieces of the 14th Indiana Battery and the two pieces attached to the 10th Missouri Cavalry. Upon receiving orders from Colonel Winslow, Captain Lee moved to the crossroads at Brice's house. It was around 11:00 a.m. when Lee examined the ground before him. After much examination, he found no advanced position that was advantageous. The best place for the work of artillery was Brice's Crossroads.[114]

Chapter 4

"You Cannot Hurry Me
or My Men Into This Fight"

Brice's Crossroads was a high piece of ground in an open area. Although it had been cleared for the house, it was also found that the ground "to the rear, left and left front, descending considerably from our position. To the right and the right front the ground was more on a level with our position." Here, Captain H.S. Lee and his Union artillerymen found themselves surrounded by "dense timber, dense woods and thicket, the roads being the only openings." Of concern was the fact that the woods were very near his artillery. Considering the topography and denseness of the woods, Confederates could move practically undetected, thus allowing the attacking enemy to approach the guns through the woods and avoid the roads altogether. It was possible for the enemy to get within one hundred to fifty yards before the artillery might be alerted to their whereabouts. In being able to see the enemy, Lee would admit that he could but "only from the position of my left piece, the extreme left piece of all that were on the hill. The others were fired by guess-work, by information gained by going to the front, and by reports from the front." Quickly, Lee placed the 7th Wisconsin Battery "on the left of the main road, and on this side of and very near to the Baldwyn road." The 14th Indiana Battery had its guns situated "on the left of the main road, immediately on the other side of the Baldwyn road." Finally, the guns of the 10th Missouri Cavalry were positioned "just at the intersection of the two roads, just to the right of the main road." In doing so, these guns were situated so that they could sweep the fields before them.[115]

The question was whether Lee and his men would see the Confederates coming, if and when they did.

Not far from Lee and his artillery, Rucker and his men of Mississippi and Tennessee readied themselves for the fight ahead. It was around noon, and the men on both sides of the fight were feeling the heat, but there was little time to think about that. The order had come to charge, and the men of Rucker's brigade wasted no time in following their orders. These men were heading in the direction of the Union line that included the 7th Indiana Cavalry, and to that regiment's right could be found the 2nd New Jersey Cavalry, followed to their right by a battalion of the 3rd Iowa Cavalry on the right of the Guntown road and the 4th Iowa Cavalry Regiment to their right and then a battalion under Major Jones of the 3rd Iowa, which included companies F, G, H and I, on the right of the 4th Iowa. In doing so, the 3rd Iowa was separated by the 4th Iowa, which was between the two 3rd Iowa battalions. Hurrying to the battlefield, Rucker's men now found the enemy occupying the woods "on the far side of the field," as John Preston Young of the 7th Tennessee Cavalry remembered, "with a thicket fence greatly strengthened with rails and logs and garnished with an abates of such bushy trees as could be cut across the fence." The field before them included a gully, which was parallel to the advancing line, with the ditch bisecting the 7th Tennessee Cavalry, which had formed "across and on either side of it."[116]

Rucker and his field officers were mounted as they and the dismounted cavalrymen moved through the knee-high corn. Riding also made the officers conspicuous targets, and halfway through the field, many of them became dismounted owing to their horses being shot out from under them. The Union line was easy to see. William Witherspoon of the 7th Tennessee Cavalry recalled, "Nearing the opposite side of the field we discovered the yanks had doubled down the rail fence with logs on top, behind which the yanks were lying, with a bright line of steel shining in front…Just in front of us was a slight rise thinly covered with broom-sedge." The word had gone down the line to fall on the ground after the first flash of the Union guns and then to rise with a yell and a volley and cross over the fence. As Rucker's men got upon the rise, it was heard from the Union line, "Make ready! Take aim! Fire!" In this volley alone, the Tennesseans lost 75 killed and disabled to where they were no longer able to fight in the war. Out of about 350 soldiers, many others received temporary wounds.[117]

Interestingly, this ploy by the 7th Tennessee Cavalry to lie on the ground when the Union men fired had an effect on at least one cavalryman of the 3rd Iowa, who admitted to a Confederate soldier much later, "with our guns pointed through the fence, taking good aim on your advancing line—we will kill every man in that line. At the word fire, we poured a deadly volley into you, and as we expected, you all fell and we were sure that we had completely wiped you from the face of the earth." The Iowan added, "But to our surprise and astonishment, it seemed that the dead line had bounded to their feet with double the number, yelling and shooting like mad devils."[118]

Rucker's brigade continued to move forward through the muddy field of corn, but now the fence and abatis on the Union line "were ablaze with the fire of the enemy's breech-loaders, and the men began to fall thickly on the field. The fire was terrible from this invisible foe, and the regiment was staggered." Private John Milton Hubbard of the 7th Tennessee Cavalry stated later, "It looked like death to go to the fence, but many of the men reached it." This hail of fire was too much for many in the 7th Tennessee as they dropped to the ground and sought shelter in any gully that was nearby. Lieutenant Colonel Taylor would have none of this as he rode down the line ordering the men to their feet and to charge forward. Encouraged, the regiment let out a great cheer and rushed forward to the slope before the enemy line, "leaving," as Young recalled, "the ground strewed with fallen comrades in their rear." "The roar of artillery and the fusillade of small arms were deafening," recalled Private Hubbard. "Sheets of flame were along both lines while dense clouds of smoke arose above the heavily wooded field." Hubbard would fail to remember just how many times the gray line surged at this moment in the battle, only to conclude, "I cannot now say how many times this was repeated, for men in the very presence of death take no note of time."[119] Both sides had worn out the other. In what appeared to Hubbard to be "common consent," both sides "drew back just far enough for the intervening trees and dense undergrowth to obscure the vision." The Confederates rested on the ground still in line of battle. Water for the 7th Tennessee was in great supply, for they were near "a bountiful supply of water from the rills, which had been fed by the recent rains." Hubbard would recall, "I never tasted better."[120]

While the firing was fierce along the 3rd and 4th Iowa line, Private Joseph McCaulley of Company E, 3rd Iowa Cavalry, recalled that the regiments "were dismounted and advanced into a thick wood or rather thick underbrush where we found the enemy posted in force and a brisk action soon commenced the heaviest of the enemys fire falling on the 4th Iowa cav but was answered with such a destructive fire from the Spencer Carbines in the hands of the 4th cav that they were forced to fall back in considerable disorder." Rucker's men didn't fall back too far, for McCaulley remembered that they were "not out of hearing as we could plainly hear the officers giving orders."[121] Captain Eldred Huff, writing of the 4th Iowa Cavalry, Company A, in 1882, agreed as he remembered that his men "formed on the left of the main road and on a high ridge where we were well protected not only by the natural lay of the ground, but also by heavy timber. Here the enemy charge us twice and were repulsed each time with great loss. This position—with our breech loading carbines, we could have held until now."[122]

Lyon's Kentuckians had been so impressed with how well Rucker's men were doing as dismounted fighters that Hord recalled, "We, having served as infantry, were agreeably surprised to see him with his dismounted cavalry keep up his side so well; and all day long, when Rucker got 'busy,' our boys would shout out: 'O, my Rucker,' 'Stay with him, Rucker. Even when we had trouble of our own in front, we found time to cheer Rucker."[123] This may have helped the 7th Tennessee Cavalry; however, the 18th Mississippi Cavalry on the left of the Confederate line was having problems of its own.

The 18th Mississippi Cavalry also moved with the 7th Tennessee; however, the 18th Mississippi did not have support on its left flank and was overlapped by enemy forces. Due to the fact that the 18th Mississippi's left flank was "in the air," it opened itself up to a terrible enfilading fire from the Iowan troops. Once this happened, the Mississippians broke and retreated toward the woods in their rear for cover. These troops, which had only 225 effective that day, regrouped and moved forward once again to face the enemy.[124]

As the men of the 7th Tennessee Cavalry continued their push against the 7th Indiana Cavalry, the men of the 18th Mississippi found themselves back in the fight and a little more careful as they approached Winslow's line. This time, the two battalions of the 4th Iowa Cavalry to their front were posted among an oak thicket, except for the area that the Guntown road passed through. Here, the Iowans heard the Mississippians, but they could not see them well. As the Iowans listened to the crash of battle taking place to their left, they desperately examined the area to their front, questioning what and who it could be. In no time, the 18th Mississippi was upon them. This time, the Mississippians took cover and poured a leaden storm into the Iowans. The Mississippians' object of the battle was to keep the 4th Iowans busy. By doing so, the men of the 18th helped to keep part of the Union line from performing an enfilading fire into the rest of the Confederate line.[125]

As Grierson's cavalry was being held under attack, Sturgis found himself waiting for the pioneer corps and examining the quagmire of a road that led through Hatchie Bottom. It was here, earlier in the morning, that Lieutenant Colonel John W. Noble of the 3rd Iowa Cavalry recalled, "We crossed a swamp, or bayou, very difficult of passage, and which was not bridged. A man on horseback found great difficulty in getting over, and one horse of this command was suffocated in the mud." Delays and difficulties were quite possibly weighing on Sturgis's mind when one of Grierson's men rode up with a message from Grierson with the time of 10:00 a.m. Grierson mentioned that he had taken a crossroads leading to Baldwyn and that an enemy picket had "attempted to destroy a bridge, but did not succeed." Grierson went on to explain that he had halted to wait on orders and went on to explain that Forrest and Roddey were to join at one point. Interestingly, he ended by stating, "Courier from the advance on the Baldwin road, just in, reports skirmishing."[126] Grierson believed shortly after the battle that he "communicated with General Sturgis and informed him that I had an advantageous position and could hold it if the infantry was brought up promptly." However, Sturgis recalled that the message from Grierson was "to the effect that his advance was engaged with a party of the enemy on the Baldwin road at Brice's Cross-Roads, some four miles in the advance of where I was." He admitted, "I paid but little attention to this as I was expecting to meet the enemy's cavalry at every moment."[127]

Not long after Sturgis received the message, another messenger came upon him from Grierson. This time, Grierson announced that the enemy was "600 strong, and that he [General Grierson] occupied a good position and a very important one, being at the cross-roads." Sturgis needed to take a look at the situation for himself. He wrote Grierson to leave between six and seven hundred of his cavalry on the Guntown road near Brice's Crossroads. This cavalry would help lead the infantry toward Guntown while Grierson took the rest of his men and forced his way to Baldwyn, driving the enemy before him. At that point, Grierson would move on Guntown by way of the railroad. Sturgis added, "I didn't propose to allow the enemy to draw me from my main line of march." Just then, Colonel McMillen arrived in advance of his infantry forces. This was a perfect opportunity for delegation. After explaining to McMillen the need for fixing the morass-laden area in the road immediately, Sturgis rode off to Brice's Crossroads.[128]

Interestingly, the same Sturgis who didn't believe that Grierson's troops were facing great odds would later recall that as he made his way toward the crossroads, he became aware of the possibility that Grierson may not know just exactly what he was up against. The enemy could be in greater numbers than Grierson thought. Therefore, Sturgis sent an aide back to McMillen, directing him to "send forward the advance brigade of infantry to Brice's Cross-Roads as rapidly as possible without distressing his men."

Once again, as Sturgis continued his ride, an aide came from Grierson with another message. This time, there was an air of urgency: "The enemy was in considerable force, and that he had nearly all his command engaged." This alarmed Sturgis enough to have him order McMillen requesting "to lose no time in getting up." According to Sturgis, he arrived at the crossroads at 12:00 p.m.[129] What Sturgis found was the tyranny of the urgent. "When I reached the crossroads I found nearly all the cavalry engaged, and the battle growing warm, but no artillery had yet opened on either side."[130]

Grierson tended to see the situation differently than Sturgis. From what Grierson recalled, after his troops had been engaged with the Confederate forces for at least two hours, it was Sturgis's adjutant, Captain Rawolle, who appeared and explained that Sturgis believed that Grierson was fighting a force of brigade strength from 1,200 to 1,500 men. Furthermore, Grierson was to continue to move on toward Baldwyn while leaving a detachment of cavalry at Brice's Crossroads until the infantry arrived, at which point the infantry would proceed toward Guntown. Grierson tried to explain that the Baldwyn road was blocked. He even escorted the captain to the area where the fighting was still heavy so that he could witness for himself that the struggle was greater than Sturgis believed. Needless to say, Captain Rawolle understood the situation quite well, including the close approximation of the enemy, when the heel of his boot was shot off. Upon Rawolle's discovery of the situation, "He wheeled his horse and rapidly returned to the general, impressed with the idea, I presume, that it was a difficult matter to travel out from there on the road to Baldwyn."[131]

According to Grierson, it was around 1:00 p.m. when Sturgis arrived at the battlefield, along with his staff and the 19th Pennsylvania Cavalry as his escort. Sturgis had a lot to take in once he examined the area around him. Confusion seemed to reign as he noticed that a section of a battery of artillery was not in position. Furthermore, along the crossroads could be found artillery, ambulances and horses that Sturgis believed "jammed in the road, and my first attention was directed to clearing the road, so that the infantry could get up." Sturgis still believed the enemy was only cavalry. Although the rifle fire was, according to Sturgis, "pretty heavy, but no artillery had opened on either side, which led me to believe that probably the force in front of us was nothing but the enemy's cavalry, as I had no information to lead me to believe otherwise."[132]

True, it was Confederate cavalry, but Sturgis had underestimated his opponent. It would seem that Sturgis did arrive at 1:00 p.m., as Grierson reported, instead of 12:00 p.m., as Sturgis stated. Forrest recalled that the heavy skirmish was kept up until 1:00 p.m. This was about the time that Buford finally arrived, accompanied by Morton's artillery and Bell's brigade close behind. While Sturgis was correct that heavy firing was heard, no Confederate cannon were fired due to the fact that they had not arrived yet. Also, Union cannon had bellowed out to the Confederates long before Sturgis's arrival to the crossroads, as Forrest was a witness, recalling, "The enemy had for some time been shelling our position." It is possible that Sturgis had just arrived at a lull in the battle, with its greatest fury to follow soon after his arrival.[133]

In seeing the situation around Grierson's battle line, an excited Sturgis headed toward the Ripley road, stating within earshot of Grierson, "If the damned cavalry could only be gotten out of the way," he could "soon whip the enemy with his infantry." Grierson was indignant at this remark. He believed the cavalry had fought a good fight, and he had only asked for a brigade of infantry. Now he was left to wonder why this infantry brigade was still not on the battlefield.[134] Regardless, Grierson kept asking Sturgis when the infantry would replace his cavalrymen and also reminded Sturgis that the troops had been fighting for hours and that they were probably low on ammunition. Sturgis assured the cavalryman that the infantry was indeed close by and would be there soon, assuring that the ammunition could not nearly be all used up just yet. Now Sturgis started receiving requests from all sides. Waring and Winslow sent their requests for relief directly to Sturgis, with Winslow explaining that his troops were "hard pressed." Turning to Grierson, Sturgis directed him to gather "all of the idle men about the crossroads, of which there were a great many, and skulkers, and put them into the fight where they were the most needed."[135]

Sturgis now turned to the artillery at the crossroads. Here, he ordered one section of the artillery to fire on the Confederate reserves that could be seen. Firing into the woods might have played havoc with Union troops, since it was impossible to see the opposing lines. More calls were coming in for Sturgis to bring forward any reinforcements, but he couldn't. The infantry was on its way, but relief was needed now. The battle situation made Winslow and his line exceedingly volatile. He had been nervously asking for relief, and Sturgis began to have the idea that Winslow just might pull out of line without authority. If so, it could jeopardize the Guntown road and the Union right line of defense. Instead, Sturgis directed Winslow that in case he were to be overrun by the Confederate forces, he should fall back slowly in the direction of the crossroads. This would contract his line, thus giving it strength. While plugging this possible hole in the line, Sturgis became alarmed with the Union left under Waring. Sturgis would later recall, "Through some misunderstanding that I am yet unable to explain, the cavalry had been withdrawn without my knowledge from the left, and I was compelled to occupy the line temporarily with my escort, consisting of about 100 of the Nineteenth Pennsylvania Cavalry." In actuality, Waring, not getting the infantry support he so desperately needed, was finally forced to fall back about two hundred feet, where he also formed a new line. In doing so, this caused Winslow's brigades to correct themselves by retiring so that it continued to connect with Waring. In other words, they did as Sturgis had mentioned: fall back to a more constricted line, thereby strengthening the line in the process. Sturgis believed it was around 1:30 p.m. when the infantry started to arrive on the field. Little did he know that Forrest's major push was just beginning.[136]

While Sturgis was trying to take in the situation surrounding him at Brice's Crossroads, McMillen had his hands full trying to move the infantry and wagon train toward and through Hatchie Bottom. McMillen, like everyone else, found it "impossible to put it in good condition." No doubt frustrated with the site of water and deep mud, McMillen waited in front of his column in anticipation as to when he would hear from the rear of his wagon train. Soon a courier rode up from the front with a message from Sturgis stating that Grierson "had struck the enemy beyond Brice's Crossroads, some five miles in advance." McMillen was ordered to move his leading brigade "up as rapidly as possible to the support of the cavalry, leaving the other two brigades to come up with the train." Suddenly, priorities had changed for the commander of the infantry division. He quickly sent Colonel George B. Hoge of the 113th Illinois Infantry and commander of the Second Brigade forward. This made the most sense, as Hoge's brigade was in the advance this day. McMillen, who was mounted, had the men move forward at "quick time." No longer was he to worry about the rear of the train and the Hatchie Bottom quicksand; instead, he sent his quartermaster to close up the wagons and to direct the brigades under Wilkin and Bouton to move forward as quickly as possible. McMillen moved out with the Second Brigade.[137]

As McMillen and his lead brigade moved toward Brice's Crossroads, the stress of urgency continued to meet him in the form of couriers coming from the battlefield with many repeated orders "to move up as rapidly as possible as the enemy was developing a large force and driving our cavalry back." The Second Brigade included tough westerners of the 81st, 95th, 108th, 113th and 120th Illinois Infantry Regiments, along with Company B, 2nd Regiment Illinois Artillery, under the command of Captain F.H. Chapman.[138]

"You Cannot Hurry Me or My Men Into This Fight"

According to Hoge, the command had left camp around 10:00 a.m. that morning, and although Hatchie Bottom was a problem, he managed to get his men in good order. He believed that it was around 1:00 p.m. when he received word from McMillen to "move forward instantly, as General Grierson was fighting and hotly pressed. I moved at once." Soon after this, Hoge was met with another message. This time, McMillen advised that he would be moving forward with his escort at a "gait as he thought the infantry could march." However, if this was too quick for the troops on foot, he should just send word forward. This "gait" was kept up for two and a half miles, or about the time five men of the 113th Illinois Infantry succumbed to heat stroke. This was too much, and McMillen was advised of the situation. Finally, the men were halted along a stream long enough to fill their canteens and catch their breaths. Now, Hoge received another message from McMillen stating, "Move forward as rapidly as possible, as the enemy were gaining ground, and the only thing that would save us was the infantry." The men were now at a quick march until within about three-quarters of a mile of the battlefield.[139]

The heat was getting the best of many a soldier that day. J.H. Mooney of Company E, 113th Illinois Infantry, would remember this day for many years to come, stating, "The air was hot close and oppressive. The sun seemed to be drawing down heat like a blast furnace. The men kept up well until within about 3 or 4 miles of the battle field, they then commenced falling at nearly every hundred feet by over heat sun stroke & want of water, they would take 2 or 3 stagering steps, fall down and commence crying & calling for water." Mooney continued, "We would tair their shirt collars open, pour water on their neck, & heads carrie them to a shade tree & runn for our place in the ranks."[140]

Lieutenant Colonel George R. Clark, also of the 113th Illinois Infantry, was ordered to move his command at the double-quick and did so for about four miles, only to find that "one-third of my men were so completely exhausted as to be scarce able to stand; several were sun-struck." Tempers were also heated as officers such as Colonel Humphrey of the 95th Illinois Infantry realized the fatigue the men were feeling and refused to force his men to double-quick. Instead, they moved at a quick march. J. Barber, an adjutant of the 95th Ohio Infantry whose post was with Colonel McMillen this hot June day, was busy as the staff officer of the division, directing the regimental commanders as to where their men should be in line of battle. Now, Barber was sent back by order of Sturgis to "hurry them up to double-quick." Upon delivering the order to Humphrey, the exasperated colonel barked out, "Lieutenant, you can place me in arrest, but you cannot hurry me or my men into this fight." Regardless, the men still continued to fall by the roadside. Barber lamented, "I saw hundreds of good soldiers so tired out with the double quick march as to be unable to load their guns when they got there."[141]

Other commanders within the brigade felt the heat of the day and the heat from their commanders. Colonel Franklin Campbell of the 81st Illinois Infantry moved his men forward as ordered. However, "very soon orders came to double-quick the men, as moments were everything." Campbell continued to receive "orders upon orders, that I hurried and urged the men forward a distance of four miles under hot sun to the field of battle." The situation was difficult and only got worse. "As I rode along the moving column from regiment to regiment," recalled Dr. L. Dyer, surgeon in chief to the infantry and artillery, "and saw the numerous cases of sunstroke, and the scores and hundreds of men, many of them known to me as good and true soldiers, falling out by the way, utterly powerless to move forward, it was a sad, a fearful reflection, that this condition of so many, would insure a certain defeat, and terrible disaster."[142] Regardless, those who could kept marching toward the sound of the guns.

The harsh conditions were no different for the First Brigade, which followed behind Hoge and his men. These men were not ordered to start out as rapidly as the Second Brigade due to orders requesting them not to leave the supply wagons. Colonel Alexander Wilkin of the 9th Minnesota Infantry led the First Brigade. His troops consisted of veterans in the 72nd and 95th Ohio Infantry, 9th Minnesota Infantry, 114th Illinois Infantry and 93rd Indiana Infantry, along with Company E, 1st Illinois Light Artillery, and a section of the 6th Indiana Battery.[143] These men were moving at a rapid pace, which caused Sergeant John W. Lacock of the 93rd Indiana, Company C, to recall, "A burning sun was pouring down, and we shut in by a heavy growth of timber, entirely cutting off all air, the terrible suffering of men who only heard an order but to obey, with heavy loads to carry-musket, cartridge-box with forty rounds, canteen, haversack and knapsack—the inhumanity of the order will become apparent." The men could endure the pace for only so long before they began dropping out of line due to exhaustion, while others, according to Lacock, were "never to rise again, completely stricken by the intense heat, intensified by our unusual exertion." The quick pace was finally reduced to a walk as the men struggled to move forward. The walk would be short-lived, for Wilkin received word that the Second Brigade was being "severely pressed." He asked for and received permission to move his men out "more rapidly," thus leaving the supply train in the protective hands of the Third Brigade. The First Brigade moved to the double-quick for the next mile until they reached Brice's Crossroads, at which time, according to Wilkin, it was 1:30 p.m.[144]

Colonel Edward Bouton commanded the Third Brigade, which was composed of two infantry regiments and a battery of artillery. All of its men were of African descent. Upon leaving their morning camp, the men of the 55th U.S. Colored Infantry were distributed throughout the supply train, with three to four soldiers to each wagon. Battery F of the 2nd U.S. Artillery followed the train, and finally, the 59th U.S. Colored Infantry protected the rear. The Third Brigade and supply train had their own battle early on with the elements of Hatchie Bottom. The men found themselves moving the wagons at a "slow and irregular" pace through an area that was "very deep and miry." However, once out of the bottom area, the wagons finally encountered good roads. The once strung-out train could now close up, but it also called for everyone to move out rapidly with no rest breaks along the way. Lieutenant Colonel Robert Cowden commanded the 59th U.S. Colored Troops, which were to the rear of the entire infantry column, including the supply train. Soon after leaving Hatchie Bottom, Cowden recalled hearing the thunder of cannons to his front. It wasn't long before Cowden received orders from Bouton to keep closed up with the train, for a Confederate attack might be forthcoming. The march continued toward the battlefield when Bouton ordered Cowden to "close up the troops and bring them forward at double-quick to this point. Many of them double-quicked two or three miles."[145] What the last of Sturgis's infantry brigade was about to see and participate in would leave an indelible mark on the survivors.

Chapter 5

"Everything Was Going to the Devil as Fast as It Possibly Could"

Although mud-spattered and worn-out, Morton's artillery and Bell's brigade were spoiling for a fight. Union artillery had been raining down on the Confederate line for some time, and Forrest had had enough. Now with Morton's firepower at his disposal, Forrest directed Buford to get the artillery in position and open fire. Unlike the Union leadership, Forrest had a good understanding of where the Union artillery where. Now he wanted to "develop the position of enemy's batteries and his lines." Morton with his four guns, along with Rice and his four guns, moved off the Baldwyn road to the right and were put into position in an open field. From here, they kept up a rapid shelling on the area of Brice's Crossroads. Only two guns from the Union line responded. However, so far and extreme was Tyler's position, connected on the left of Rucker's line, that Tyler and his men were almost caught in friendly fire. It just so happened that Morton had begun firing his "bull pups" at two Union artillery guns protecting the crossroads when Tyler's troopers "made a diversion which brought him within immediate range of the Confederate artillery. Captain Morton discovered his identity, however, before any damage had been done, and ordered the artillery to cease firing until Captain Tyler and his men were safely out of the way."[146]

Tyler and his men were nowhere near out of harm's way. While in position on the Guntown road, what appeared to be a Union brigade was moving at the double-quick down the road toward them. If allowed, these troops could flank Rucker's men, thus throwing the Confederate left into chaos before Bell and his men could arrive. Thinking quickly, Tyler formed his men "across the road, six line deep, my flanks extending into the black-jack timber, which fortunately came near the road on each side." Although Tyler only had two companies at his disposal, the environment helped to mask the lack of troops and firepower of the Kentuckians. The Confederates opened fire on the advancing columns, thus causing the Federals to halt, form across the road and advance through the timber and upon the road in line of battle. It was at this time that Forrest and the 16th Tennessee Cavalry appeared and Tyler learned that the Confederate advance was about to begin that would encompass the entire Confederate line. Tyler was to dismount his men and continue to cover the extreme left flank. Soon after, as the men began the advance, Tyler recalled that he was struck by a spent ball on "my instep...I thought my foot was torn to pieces; I dropped my pistol and grabbed my foot. General Forrest was about ten steps away behind an old house. He galloped up to me and asked if I was much hurt. I said, 'It hurts like hell, General, but I do not see any blood or bones.' He said, 'You aren't hurt much; come on'— and I did." Soon after this, the Union soldiers were run out of the blackjack in Tyler's front.[147] Duff's 8th Mississippi Cavalry, along with Forrest's escort of about one hundred strong, was to the right of Tyler's command as the Union cavalry made its way down the Guntown road toward them.

Bell recalled, before moving his brigade to the Confederate far left, that Forrest came to him with Captain Tom Henderson and Forrest's aide-de-camp, Major Anderson, to have Bell send one of his regiments to the rear of the Union army stating, "Therefore I ordered Col. Barteau with the 2nd Tennessee to move around the enemy, so as not to be discovered and reach the rear of their wagon train as quick as possible." Forrest discontinued the artillery fire and ordered Lyon and Johnson to move their men forward. All the Confederate forces that Forrest could depend on were now on the battle line.[148]

It was 1:00 p.m., according to Forrest, and he wasted no time in moving forward to attack the Union line. Forrest had Lyon's and Johnson's troops ready to move forward. Now he turned to his escort, along with Bell's brigade, and moved quickly around to the Guntown and Ripley Road. By advancing to the road, Forrest was able to dismount the brigade, at which point he placed the 16th Tennessee Cavalry Regiment to the right, followed by the 20th Tennessee across the road, thus extending Rucker's left. He then placed the 19th Tennessee Cavalry Regiment on the left of the road. The 8th Mississippi Cavalry of Rucker's command, along with Forrest's escort, was placed to the left of the 19th Tennessee Cavalry Regiment, thus overlapping the Guntown road. Finally, Captain Henry A. Tyler's A and C Companies of the 12th

Kentucky Cavalry formed the extreme left of Forrest's line of battle.[149] As Forrest rode down the line, Hubbard of the 7th Tennessee Cavalry recalled Forrest "mounted on his big sorrel horse, sabre in hand, sleeves rolled up, his coat lying on the pommel of his saddle, looking the very God of War." Forrest shouted to the men, "Get up, men. I have ordered Bell to charge on the left. When you hear his guns, and the bugle sounds, every man must charge, and we will give them hell."[150]

Time was not with the Union army this day. McMillen had stopped his lead regiments about a mile and a half from the fighting in order to allow them much-needed rest and to fill their canteens in the misnomer branch known as Dry Creek. Now, McMillen received another frantic message to "move the brigade up in quick time without halting for any purpose whatever." This was passed to Hoge while McMillen and his staff rode to the battlefield to ascertain the situation. What McMillen found at the crossroads took him by surprise: "Everything was going to the devil as fast as it possibly could." Waring rode up, asking the bewildered colonel when his men would appear and anxiously explaining that his men could only hold the line for a matter of seconds. McMillen's answer was quick and to the point. He could not guarantee his troops in seconds; however, they should make the field within ten to fifteen minutes. The situation at the crossroads must have appeared surreal. McMillen observed all around the crossroads that "the cavalry were falling back rapidly in disorder and the roads at Brice's house were filled with retreating cavalry, led horses, ambulances, wagons, and artillery, the whole presenting a scene of confusion and demoralization anything but cheering to troops just arriving." To add to the scene, McMillen wrote, "the enemy was also shelling this point vigorously at this time and during the arrival of my troops." McMillen became a magnet for Union commanders who were frequently demanding to know when the infantry would arrive.[151]

McMillen didn't need to worry about how cheerful the infantry would be seeing the crossroads in such disarray. These infantrymen were not only worn out and thirsty, but they also found that near the end of their double-quick march was included a difficult incline rising from Tishomingo Creek to the crossroads. The march had been an ordeal many would never forget, but it was only the beginning. Regardless, Union Colonel Hoge had finally made it to the fight at what McMillen remembered as being "between 1 and 2 p.m." These men went straight into the action on the right of the Baldwyn road, thus relieving Colonel Waring's cavalry brigade. At this point in the fighting, with the 7th Indiana's right being bent and broke, they were now within a short distance of Brice's house and the crossroads. Although the

113th Illinois and the rest of Hoge's Second Brigade came up, it was a pitiful site. Hoge would later recall that when the 113th Illinois Infantry arrived, "about half of them had been left on the road, and those who remained were about exhausted. The tongues of many hung out of their mouths, and they couldn't bite a cartridge."[152] The 113th Illinois was the first infantry regiment to be placed in the line of battle with its left on the Baldwyn road, with the 120th Illinois Infantry to the right of the 113th Illinois. The 108th Illinois came up and was to the right of the 120th Illinois, with the 95th Illinois Infantry with its right covered by the left of the 81st Illinois Infantry. From here, a cavalry regiment was to the right of the 81st Illinois, which completed the Union line from the Baldwyn road. Battery B of the 2nd Illinois Artillery positioned its four guns at the crossroads. These guns were immediately put into action, with the artillerists using shells that had been fused for three to five seconds each. However, one of these guns would be moved under McMillen's orders down the Baldwyn road east toward the enemy about four hundred yards.[153]

Wilkin recalled bringing the First Brigade to Brice's Crossroads around 1:30 p.m. McMillen knew exactly where he wanted these men to make their stand and led the 95th Ohio back down the road, back down the hill

The area of the battlefield from the south viewing north between the Union infantry and Confederate lines. The low area in the middle was mistaken for a swamp due to heavy rains. *Courtesy of Emilee Bennett.*

and to the left of the 113th Illinois Infantry. Next, McMillen placed the 72nd Ohio Infantry and a section of the 6th Indiana Battery on the ridge near the Tishomingo Creek bridge about eight hundred yards southwest of Brice's Crossroads heading toward Ripley. Upon this ridge stood a log house that overlooked the road and fields around it. A company of the 72nd Ohio Infantry fanned out toward the woods to their front facing east, with the remainder formed in line to its left in support. This was a precarious place to be, for the woods were unmanageable and could hold any number of enemy forces. Great vigilance was expected since the Confederates could be expected to try to get around the Union left in order to reach the Federal wagon train or to cut off any Union chance of escape if needed. Captain Mueller of the 6th Indiana Battery was directed to fire into the tangled woods for good measure, hoping to check the progress of any Confederates lurking in the shadows. According to McMillen, the Union line, now replaced with the infantry, extended "in a semi-circular form in the direction of the Guntown road, relieving the cavalry as they took position."[154]

With the Union left bolstered and Waring's cavalry relieved from the line, McMillen now turned toward what remained of Winslow's cavalry over near the Guntown road. The 114th Illinois Infantry was placed to the right of Hoge's Second Brigade, thus completing the Union line to the Guntown road and the cavalry in that area. To the right of the Guntown road was the 93rd Indiana Infantry. The 9th Minnesota Infantry and Battery E of the 1st Illinois Light Artillery were held in reserve near Brice's Crossroads. Captain Fernald of the 72nd Ohio Infantry was put in charge of the skirmish line that now encompassed the First Brigade's entire line.[155]

Once the infantry regiments were in position across the Union line, skirmishers were moved forward with the warning that Confederate forces were near and to expect a heavy attack at any time. This was especially true for those of the 93rd Indiana Infantry, for according to McMillen, "it was very evident the enemy was then advancing to attack."[156] Moving the infantry into the line to replace a worn-out and exhausted cavalry with little to no ammunition was sorely needed. However, all across the Union line could be found a cavalry replaced with worn-out and exhausted infantry. Major Pierce of the 4th Iowa Cavalry prepared his men to move off the line but noticed that as the infantry moved up, "they had been so hurried through the heat that only a small part of the command was able to keep up." H. Ramsey of the 3rd Iowa Cavalry, Company I, remembered how the infantry "came to our relief, but oh, in such a plight…were evidently worn out; their organization was almost broken up from fatigue and heat…We were relieved by one of those broken down regiments, say about 300 strong." John W. Jenkins of the 9th Minnesota Infantry, Company E, admitted, "When we got to where they were fighting we were about played out and in no condition to help the other regiments, whipped and retreating." Still William Roarke of the 120th Illinois Infantry, Company F, explained, "We went into the battle not unitedly and in order, but by regiments or fragments of regiments and without time to form or even catch our exhausted breath." R.S. Patton of 114th Illinois Infantry, Company B, remembered, "He doubled quicked us about four miles through swamps to the battle fields and we was about given out when we arrived & was very hot. Some of the men scarcely able to load their guns." Even Colonel Waring would write caustically, "Our ammunition was reduced to five rounds per man, and when our battery had fired its last shot, that the infantry began to arrive, and then they came a regiment at a time, or only so fast as the Forrest mill could grind them up in detail." The Federal infantry had been through enough for one day; however, for them the day was far from over. It was true that the men, in general, were spent before they even felt the brunt of Forrest's final attack. However, these men would fight with an American spirit that has been admired throughout its history. Spent and worn out, these men were still willing to fight, and that fight came soon enough.[157]

An interesting thing now happened across the battlefield. As Forrest moved his men into line and the Federal infantry replaced the cavalry, a hush fell on the scene. From around 1:30 until 2:00 p.m., although a lone musket shot was heard here and there and a voice cried out to the foe in challenge, it was rather silent. Although it was quiet, the two armies readied themselves. The Confederate line waited for the order to move forward, and the Federals readied themselves for the oncoming flood. The humidity of that hot June day in Mississippi caused the soldiers' clothes to cling to their bodies as the heat and stress caused all to perspire. The smoke clearing over the fields revealed the undulating grounds between the two lines. The elevated ground on which the Union line was developed could be found with its fence rails and logs. Also, the view to the young woods, with their vines and entanglements, could be seen. These woods withheld the sun's rays, but the trees made the conditions stifling for the soldiers as the air refused to move. It was the calm before the storm.[158]

Forrest was known to lead by example, and he could be seen on many parts of the line when a battle was raging. Brice's Crossroads was no exception. After directing Bell and his brigade into line, Forrest gave Buford command of the Confederate right and center, which also included Morton's artillery.

Forrest explained to Buford, "The moment the attack began on the left to move the center and right rapidly forward." Forrest also realized that the Union line seemed to be massing in front of him and Bell's troops. Therefore, the left of the Union line could be expected to be weaker. If this were true, Johnson's Alabamians should be able to test this flank and crowd the Ripley-Guntown road up to Brice's Crossroads. Buford was expected to have his men push the right of the Confederate line, thus directing as much of the Union's attention in that direction, while Bell hit the Union right as hard as possible.[159] While the attack was to be led by Bell from the left, it would not be an easy task. Due to the density of the undergrowth, Bell and his men would have to advance to within thirty yards of the Federal line before they could actually launch the attack. The positive realization of the encounter for the Confederates was that Bell's troops were greatly concealed from Union forces. By being very close to the Union line and still concealed, it just might give the Confederates the element of surprise, which was so needed in battles such as these.[160]

After about three-quarters to a mile of riding southeast down a farm lane, Bell and his men came upon the Ripley-Guntown road. Here, Bell's men came to a halt. Bell, realizing the discrepancy in his numbers compared to those of the enemy, left one man of eight out of the line in order to hold the reins of the horses instead of a more common one-to-four ratio. Bell moved his men forward in order to get them into position for the general assault on the Union line. Minié balls could be seen hitting bushes and such as the men moved into position. Once Bell got his men into position, they once again moved forward. Bell and his men moved very slowly toward the Union line. Bell later wrote, "As soon as I got within reach of their lines, I commenced the fire, moving slowly all the time, firing as rapidly as I could." Not long after the line had moved forward, Captain John E. Bell was shot from his horse with a mortal wound. "I continued firing and moving, moving and firing; the mortality in my brigade, being so desperate, that if I had halted to stand and fight, I don't think there were any troops on earth that could have stood and felt the mortality without faltering," recalled Bell. Yet this was only the beginning.[161]

Bell's Tennesseans were now in close enough range to receive and give small arms fire and worse. The men in blue had also built crude makeshift breastworks and were lying behind them, waiting. Bell could see the Brice house just in the distance. The crossroads were not far away. A few more steps and down went Captain John Hibbits, fatally shot just in front of Bell. The gray line continued, but the firing on the officers on horseback continued to take its toll. Bell watched as his horse was shot, and finally, the war became more personal when his own son, Isaac T. Bell, was shot off his horse. As his son was carried from the field, Bell called upon a courier to move with all speed to Forrest. As the leaden missiles fell thick and fast around the Tennesseans, Bell sent the courier off with an emphatic request and warning: "If I did not get re-enforcements I could not stay where I was." In rapid time, the courier was back stating that Forrest said to hold the position, assuring Bell that a section of Morton's battery would be on its way as soon as it could move. Bell was confused. He couldn't understand how a section of artillery was going to help his men if they were so incredibly close to the enemy line. At this point, Bell made what he called "some very arch remark," not realizing that Forrest had arrived behind the courier. The general had heard Bell and replied, "General stay on the field; I am here and will stay as long as you live."[162]

Bell's men of Tennessee were moving against McMillen's blue line, consisting of the 114th Illinois and 93rd Indiana. Winslow was retiring his 4th and 3rd Iowa Cavalry units as McMillen was overseeing the placement of the infantry. The cavalry had moved out no more than what Winslow believed was "twenty yards in rear of the infantry line the enemy and our men commenced firing very fiercely." Winslow ordered his men to remain in position in support of the infantry and explained to McMillen that he would not withdraw his troops unless ordered due to the circumstances at hand. An aide from Winslow was sent to Sturgis to explain the situation and to request further orders, only to receive word from Sturgis to mount his men and retire at once. Winslow understood the effect such a move would cause if Sturgis's order was followed through on. Therefore, Winslow rode to Sturgis in order to explain the situation. Upon meeting Sturgis, Winslow found Grierson by his side. Both wanted to know, in an impatient tone, if Winslow's men were retiring.[163] Sturgis wanted the cavalry freed up in order to mount and protect the flanks of his army. Sturgis then asked if any cavalry units could help on the far Union line. Winslow offered the 7th Illinois and 10th Missouri Cavalry Regiments to help. These cavalry regiments consisted of about 150 men. These troops were to dismount along the Pontotoc road and help the 93rd Indiana Infantry protect the far left flank by countering Captain Tyler's squadron of 12th Kentucky Cavalry troops. This time, Winslow withdrew his command with orders to move to the west side of Tishomingo Creek. This movement took the cavalry about three-quarters of a mile to the rear of the fighting.[164]

"Everything Was Going to the Devil as Fast as It Possibly Could"

When Winslow found Sturgis with Grierson, it was not a congenial gathering between the two commanders. Each had his own agenda. Sturgis was trying to move the infantry into position, while Grierson was trying to get his men relieved after a battle they had been fighting since the morning hours. Grierson didn't like the fact that Sturgis was discussing with McMillen and, according to Grierson, "receiving and giving orders as the infantry troops were being marched forward, but mostly in the wrong direction to assist Colonel Waring in maintaining his position against the enemy." Grierson decided to step into the discussion but found Sturgis "excited and irritable in his manner, and rather briskly informed me that he had ordered Colonel McMillen to relieve Waring's brigade and directed me to withdraw the cavalry."[165] Both commanders were on edge. Grierson had also decided to remove a section of the Indiana battery away from Brice's Crossroads, much to the consternation of the commanding general. In what Grierson explained as "an excited manner," Sturgis asked the cavalry commander what he was doing. Grierson stated, "I was removing and preparing for the safety of a section of artillery that had been assigned to my command." Sturgis then ordered Grierson to leave the artillery where it was, further adding that "he would be responsible for its safety." As Winslow's 3rd and 4th Iowa Cavalry moved out, Grierson also had Winslow's artillery sent back over Tishomingo Creek to where the horses of the 10th Missouri and 7th Illinois had been sent earlier. The section of the Indiana battery stayed in place at the crossroads. The 3rd and 4th Iowa were to regroup west of the creek near the junction of the Ripley and New Albany roads. Grierson led the column away from the fighting.[166]

Meanwhile, on the Union right, Colonel DeWitt C. Thomas of the 93rd Indiana Infantry saw something rather peculiar moving across the field and "advancing upon my line, dressed in our uniform and carrying the Union flag, but firing upon us as they advanced." The advancing column fired into the 93rd Indiana, causing the Indianans to return the favor by unleashing their own leaded welcome. Colonel Thomas and Lieutenant Colonel Poole managed to stop the firing, believing that they were firing into their own men. Thomas considered that they could be Union cavalry, for many appeared to wear blue pants and coats. Thomas found out quickly that he was sadly mistaken. The men to his front consisted of Bell's 19th Tennessee Cavalry, with the 8th Mississippi Cavalry to their left. These men "poured into my ranks a murderous fire, thinning my ranks at a fearful rate. I then gave the command to my men 'to fire.'"[167]

The field southwest of Brice's Crossroads, looking south from the Pontotoc road with the Guntown road to the far left. This would have been the Union right and far right during the battle. *Author's collection.*

The fight in this area alone became a bloody microcosm of the battle, with each side taking ground and then giving ground. Confederate flank movements were met by Union changes of front, each time leaving the dead and wounded of both armies in their wake. Thomas would later admit, "Then commenced one of the hardest contested battles I have ever witnessed." The 19th Tennessee Cavalry would have probably agreed with Thomas's estimate of the fighting at this time. The Tennesseans had taken heavy gunfire from the Union line, and finally, after what Forrest called "suffering severely," the Tennesseans started breaking. Duff's 8th Mississippi, along with Forrest's escort, dismounted and charged the blue line in front of the 19th Tennessee in order to prevent a gap in the line. This proved successful, for the 19th Tennessee was able to gather its bearings. Captain Tyler of Forrest's escort had his men about a quarter mile from Brice's Crossroads when he spied an enemy brigade moving at the double-quick coming his way down the Guntown road. These were, quite possibly, the men of the 93rd Indiana. Tyler realized, "I lost here in two minutes more men killed and wounded than in all the day besides." Losses such as these could use up Tyler's force in no time and destroy any chance of holding the far left Confederate line. Tyler needed to act quickly. He ordered his men to "run to the left and jump over the fence." From here, the soldiers followed the fence line until they were clearly on the Union right flank. The rest of the 93rd Indiana was also struggling to hold the far Union right. Thomas threw out Companies A and F to the right as skirmishers in order to protect the flank while also pulling back the right wing to try to anchor that part of the line.[168]

At this point, Tyler's men fell to the ground and, "pushing our guns through the cracks near the ground, opened fire upon their flank." This completely confused the Federal troops, and their line on the right broke in confusion. Now, losses in Companies A and F of the 93rd Indiana were fearful, and officers on the line such as Poole were mortally wounded, while others were falling as well. Soon after, these men regrouped and faced Tyler's position. All looked dim for Tyler until, "to our great joy and relief," the 19th Tennessee appeared after regrouping and charged on the 93rd Indiana's flank after they had changed front to attack Tyler's men. This sent the Unionists fleeing back toward Brice's Crossroads. Incredibly, the Indianans would be able to charge again, pushing the Tennesseans back only to be outflanked and forced to retreat while firing and changing front in order to keep from being surrounded. This continued until Thomas and his men were finally pushed all the way back to Brice's house, were the artillery was also posted. Here, the Indianans made a stand as the 19th Tennessee kept up the pressure. Fortunately for Thomas, the 9th Minnesota Infantry came out of reserve and joined Thomas's line to the right.[169]

Lieutenant Colonel J.F. Marsh and the rest of the 9th Minnesota Infantry found themselves as a reserve behind the 93rd Indiana and on the left of the artillery at Brice's Crossroads. Here, they were fortunate enough to sit down and rest as they waited for orders. In a short time, McMillen rode up to Marsh and ordered him and his men to the right of the batteries and along the Guntown road where the Confederate left had been seen earlier. McMillen explained in no uncertain terms to "hold it at all hazards." The 9th Minnesota Infantry moved out, with Company D serving as skirmishers to the right of the line. This was the far right of the Union line for the infantry. According to Marsh, his regiment was to move "in line of battle and relieve the Ninety-third Indiana Infantry which had been contending against superior numbers, until nearly annihilated."[170]

Marsh recalled seeing the 93rd Indiana falling back as the 9th Minnesota moved forward. Now the 93rd Indiana was in the rear of the 9th Minnesota's left flank, believing it stayed there until ordered to fall back to support the artillery at the crossroads. Like the Indianans before them, the 9th Minnesota found that "the ground occupied by us during this engagement was so densely covered with underbrush, that major Markham and myself were compelled to dismount and send our horses to the rear until the engagement was over."

Marsh's skirmishers to the right were the first to encounter Confederate resistance, leaving a number of the Minnesotans dead and wounded. Marsh could now see the enemy line encompassing his front when a fire was let loose on the Confederates, "killing and wounding a large number." As completed before with the 93rd Indiana, the Confederates looked to flank the Union line to the right. As the fighting ebbed and flowed between both lines, the Minnesotans gave as well as they got from the 19th Tennessee, 8th Mississippi and Tyler's squadron of 12th Kentuckians. Finally, the 9th Minnesota got the upper hand and pushed the Confederate force back and "pursued him closely for about eighty rods."[171]

It would seem that the 9th Minnesota was on its way to victory except for one thing that stood in its way: the Union artillery. It was at this point, as the men were pushing the Confederates down the road and through the woods, that Marsh believed that he could have "turned his left completely, but for the grape from our own guns, which, on account of our advanced position, were now flying thick through our left flank, and had already wounded three of my men, hence we were compelled to fall back to our former position, which was done rather reluctantly." Not long after returning to the crossroads, Marsh and his men were ordered to support the battery to their left. Yet again the Southerners were coming back. Before the 9th Minnesota was "fairly engaged," Marsh was ordered to fall back, "which was done in good order for about a mile and a half." Although they had fought well, the Union line was crumbling. Colin F. MacDonald was a color-bearer for the 9th Minnesota and watched as three men of his color guard were shot in battle. He recalled, "Soon after this the regiments on the left and left center gave way, because of superior force and an attack on their flanks." Regardless, the 9th Minnesota would find itself moving through and off the battlefield without victory.[172]

Together, the 9th Minnesota and the 93rd Indiana gained back their original line, with the Confederates, according to Thomas, "giving way, left us in comparative quiet for a short time." The 93rd Indiana and 9th Minnesota had fought hard. Colonel Wilkin would write how the 9th Minnesota had "behaved splendidly, keeping a good line & driving the enemy before them, but they were too numerous and kept outflanking them." He added, "At one time about twenty of the enemy appeared suddenly in front when two companies fired killing or wounding everyone." Of the 93rd Illinois he wrote, "The Regt. Which they relieved was terribly cut up, having lost in killed alone one third of its officers." Although they had gained back the 93rd Indiana's original line, it had come with a high cost.[173]

Chapter 6

"Order Soon Gave Way to Confusion and Confusion to Panic"

The Tishomingo Creek Bridge had been a busy and important part of the battle. The infantry's arrival to the field depended on it, and as most of the soldiers had moved across and toward the sounds of battle, others also followed. As the fighting could be heard within the woods leading to Brice's house and within the area of and around the crossroads, people continued their eastward movement across the bridge. William Forse Scott, an adjutant of the 4th Iowa, examined the situation on the road and around the creek bridge: "A mixed throng still going toward the front,—soldiers singly and in squads, stragglers, camp-followers, servants,—all hurrying over the bridge and toward the cross-roads." Due to the disorder, the 3rd Iowa was delayed in crossing to the west. The men of the 4th Iowa also found themselves waiting on the east side of the creek. Finally, the 3rd Iowa was able to cross. Grierson remained near the bridge and observed, "The ammunition wagons, which had been brought forward to the vicinity of the battleground, were scattered about, mixed up with artillery and caissons and ambulances, and some of them stuck in the mud." He recalled that the supply train was still moving east and the head of the train was nearing the creek bridge, "by whose order I knew not." Most alarming was the fact that, according to Grierson, "the train occupied the road and extended back over a rising slope up to the high ground in the timber beyond, over half a mile distant."[174]

Sturgis was trying to keep the situation under control. He had managed to relieve the cavalry even though it was replaced with worn-out infantry. He worked to cover both flanks that were being threatened and posted troops near the bridge in case of an advance on the rear by Forrest's men. The cavalry was to deploy on the flanks to cover any flanking movement his infantry could not control, and the supply train was about a mile and a half away from the battlefield, or so Sturgis thought. One of the great unknowns for Sturgis and the rest of the Union troops was how many of the enemy were in the woods. They knew Confederates were within the dense foliage and thick vine-choked morass. They just couldn't decipher if it held fifteen thousand men or fifty. Early on, Sturgis feared that his "lines were giving away, though I couldn't see it, as the timber was so heavy, so I directed the commander of the battery to open his battery on the enemy's reserves."[175] In other words, Sturgis was firing blindly into the woods. Sturgis continued to control the situation along the crossroads; he was also notified that the ordnance train that had been reported to be a mile and a half away a few minutes ago was now at the bridge. Sturgis recalled, "Fearing that it might be in our way in case we were driven back I ordered it into an open field near the cavalry, there to be turned around and carried further to the rear."[176] Two main problems came with this decision to turn the wagons around in the open field. One was that the heavy rains and the field of corn made the situation look like Hatchie Bottom. Second, the wagons were easy targets for the Confederates to focus on. Sergeant John Jones of the 4th Iowa Cavalry of Company E watched as they "parked between the creek and the enemy where the mud was up to the hubs of the wagons the whole train being right under the guns of the enemy." Not long after the wagons were in this position, Jones recalled, "I saw one or two wagons struck by cannon balls before the rout began." William Scott, also of the 4th Iowa Cavalry, watched in disbelief as the wagons continued to come across the Tishomingo Creek bridge, lamenting, "They moved right on, over the bridge—a fatal bridge to many of them it was—and almost into the battlefield. Indeed the enemy's shells soon fell in the wagon-park, causing great consternation among the drivers and camp retainers." It was the beginning of the end for Sturgis's wagon train.[177] While the wagons were caught in a dilemma, the Union line around Brice's Crossroads had problems of its own.

To the left of the 93rd Indiana could be found the 114th Illinois Infantry— at least, what was left of them after the march. About one hundred men, or one-quarter, of the regiment had fallen out due to the march. The 114th Illinois now found itself to the left of the Guntown road and about 300 yards in advance of Brice's Crossroads, with the right about 150 yards from the road to Guntown. Lieutenant Colonel John F. King led the Illinoisans this day and found that he could not find Union troops to his left. A greater

The field where part of Sturgis's wagon train parked to the east of Tishomingo Creek. This photograph was taken from the top of Log Cabin Ridge looking south. *Courtesy of Emilee Bennett.*

problem was the fact that "the brush was very thick where my line was formed, and on all sides of us." Furthermore, King had been warned that there were at least two lines of Union troops to the 114th Illinois' front and to be careful about firing due to the situation. King advanced his men with the warning that Union skirmishers were to their front. King was assured by some of his men that they would not fire due to the fact that they were too tired to load their guns. King believed that he and his men had already relieved one of these lines.[178]

Occasionally, King and his officers could see men moving in their front; however, some of these men wore blue while others wore butternut. Some of the men did not want to take any chances, believing that the line should open fire. Some rationalized the situation by saying "that if they were our men they had no business to be wearing butternut clothes." Some did violate orders and fired, but most held back. In minutes, the truth revealed itself. There were no Union troops to King's front. A Confederate line moved on the Illinoisans, with King giving the order to fire. The troops in King's front most likely were Bell's Tennesseans and, more specifically, the 16th Tennessee Cavalry. These Tennesseans returned a galling fire back into the faces of the

114th Illinois at the same time. Now the fight was on, as each side exchanged lead until the gray line fell back. The Tennesseans charged again and continued to fire into the blue line. King and his men started to feel the heat not only from their front but the flanks as well. It seemed as if they would counter one flank attack and then the other flank would be hit. Adding to the reason for the flank movements was the fact that when the 93rd Indiana Infantry was pushed back, it would expose the 114th Illinois' flank, which Bell's men tried to exploit. This continued as the men moved back and near Brice's Crossroads. The Illinoisans, as King stated, "were in considerable confusion and very much exhausted." Now King and his men formed about thirty yards in front of the artillery, and he found Union troops to his left. These were the men of the 81st Illinois Infantry.[179] The men of the artillery did what they could in order to fire over the heads of the Union troops while also firing across the Guntown road. The 114th Illinois extended across the Guntown road and was in front of one of the guns, causing King to "break files on the right each time that the gun was fired. King watched as the 93rd Indiana fell back into position on his right, where it moved to the left and rear of the Brice house.[180]

It had been a difficult time for all of the forces involved along McMillen's Union right and Bell's Confederate left. The Confederate tide continued its ebb and flow, but Forrest had kept his composure when the far left looked as if it might break and when the 9th Minnesota Infantry came into action from its reserve position. Bell had been shaken but continued moving the Tennesseans forward. Forrest had assured Bell that he would stay with him, and he had. Thinking quickly, Forrest sent an aide to Buford to get Johnson's and Lyon's troops moving and to press the Union army on the Confederate right. When Forrest was not within sight, he could still be expected to be somewhere close by and along the line, pushing the men forward or leading the way. At this point, it was crucial that the men know he was with them in action. Seeing the plight of the Tennesseans, Forrest dismounted, as did his escort. After hitching their horses to nearby bushes, the group followed Forrest into "the thickest of the fray, pistol in hand, to take his place in the front rank with his men." Bell gained confidence, and together they rallied the Tennesseans and advanced on the Union line once again. Bell would later recall that it was "less than five minutes, after Forrest joined me, their line broke and we were standing so close to them that we almost made a fence with the wounded and dead as they arose to run. We pressed forward after them."[181]

The Federal line covered by the Second Brigade, commanded by Colonel Hoge, was just across from Rucker's gray line. As the men of Illinois moved

A Confederate view of the right center of the Union infantry line. The Guntown road is behind the tree line. *Courtesy of Emilee Bennett.*

The area where Bell's Tennesseans attacked on the Confederate left. The cemetery is to the right across the Baldwyn road, with Brice's Crossroads to the center and behind the tree line. *Courtesy of Emilee Bennett.*

forward into position, Rucker unleashed the 7th Tennessee Cavalry and 18th Mississippi Cavalry to cover the area near Bell's Tennessee brigade. It was at this same moment that Forrest was with Bell in their struggle for the left. As the Union line moved forward with "bayonets fixed," Rucker reminded the men with a shout, "Kneel on the ground, men, draw your six-shooters, and don't run!" Hubbard of the 7th Tennessee moved out with the Mississippians, "advancing over the dead bodies of Federals and Confederates and regaining the ground lost in the last repulse." Continuing on, he found "small bushes, cut off near the ground and falling in our front, meant that the Federals had been reinforced by veteran infantry and were firing low." The men of the 18th Mississippi understood fighting and war. Sergeant Columbus K. Hall had come from a long line of fighters and had fought earlier in the war with the 39th Alabama Regiment. His name had also been added to the esteemed *Roll of Honor* for his valor in the Battle of Murfreesboro. Yearning to join a cavalry regiment, he now served under Forrest. However, Brice's Crossroads was to be his last battle. In the constant movement of the fighting, young Hall fell with a mortal wound to the head. That day, Hall, like many of his comrades, would pay the ultimate price for his Southern homeland. He was a leader of valor, and like so many others who were lost to the Confederacy this day, Forrest, could ill afford to lose them. As the Mississippians continued to move forward, the battle continued at different points on the line. The fight was exceptionally fierce, with hand-to-hand fighting along with bayonets and navy sixes.

At one point, Hoge recalled while being on the skirmish line during this fight that "our men captured the flag of a Mississippi regiment, we were in such close quarters." Not long after this, the Union line found itself moving back due in part to a flanking fire coming from its left. Lyon's and Johnson's men were making good on their part of the battle from the cover of the woods.[182]

Now that Forrest had helped lead Bell's men back into the fight and Rucker's men were in action and pressing the enemy, Forrest wondered what was happening on the lines under Buford's control. He feared that the order sent to the general may have "miscarried." Forrest moved rapidly down the

Columbus K. Hall, 18th Mississippi Cavalry. *Private collection of Russell Hall.*

The thick brush area in front of the Union infantry line with a view to the east and south, from where Rucker's brigade attacked. *Courtesy of Emilee Bennett.*

lines, encouraging the men as he went until he finally met with Buford. It was here that he believed that only two guns of the artillery were engaged in the battle. This was unacceptable. Forrest ordered the artillery to be brought forward and ordered Buford to get it immediately brought into action. His order, of course, was followed immediately.[183]

As Bell's forces continued to force their way along the Confederate left, Colonel Hoge, commanding the Second Brigade of the infantry division, watched Rucker's line across the way. Hoge could also see what appeared to be Bell's brigade moving to the right and toward the rear of his line. Hoge immediately returned to Brice's Crossroads and had a section of artillery fire five-second shells in Bell's direction. After examining the situation around him, it was perfectly clear to Hoge that the movement toward the Union right flank was indeed a feint. Instead, he believed that the main objective was to turn the Union left flank and reach the rear of the Federal line. This opinion fell on Sturgis's and McMillen's deaf ears. It wasn't long before Hoge's skirmishers were driven in and the Union line was engulfed in battle. Hoge called on the artillery to set their shells for three seconds, but they were firing blind. Although the artillery was posted on open ground, they were close to the woods. Furthermore, the battery couldn't even see its own infantry to the front. Hoge later admitted, "The enemy could not be seen at a greater distance than twenty yards from our line or our skirmishers, owing to the dense growth of timber and underbrush."[184] It only got worse for Hoge's men on this line as the fighting continued. On the far right of Hoge's line could be found the 81st Illinois Infantry.

The 81st Illinois had problems of its own. After marching in the hot sun like the rest of the infantry, the 81st reached its destination in the line of battle. Colonel Franklin Campbell admitted, "I was forced to put the regiment in line in an open space of ground without a leaf of shade, when numbers of them fell down exhausted from over-exertion under the terrible heat." John Bartleson of the regiment recalled, "The right of our regiment was on the edge of woods on the south. Other regiments of the brigade were stationed along the fence running north and along a fence bearing off slightly to the northeast." Campbell moved his skirmishers out as quickly as possible. These men had advanced only a short distance when they were hit with the main Confederate line. This was made possible due to the "heavy timber with thick undergrowth" to the right and front of the 81st Illinois. Even the heat of battle could not subside the arguments of siblings within the ranks. John Bartleson's eldest brother, Edwin, then a sergeant with the 81st Illinois Regiment, came to John to remind him, "Johnnie, you must stand up to the works. Some of the men have shown the white feather." To this, John blurted out, "Ed,

A view looking toward Hoge's Union infantry line. Many of Lyon's Kentuckians would have followed this path. Also, Rucker's brigade would have shared much of this view. The Baldwyn road is to the right. Brice's Crossroads is to the upper right. The present-day church can be seen in the tree line. *Author's collection.*

An area considered "swampy," with high brush and grass, in front of the Union infantry line viewed from the Baldwyn road looking south and west toward the Guntown road behind the tree line. *Courtesy of Emilee Bennett.*

you attend to your business and I will attend to mine." John could see "the skirmish line came rushing back and the bullets began whizzing past." The Confederate troops of the 20th Tennessee Cavalry made several charges but were pushed back. John Bartleson readied himself for the fight and fired on his foe. However, he found that "my gun burst the cap but did not shoot. I hammered on the breech of the gun to prime it or jar some powder in the tube…the gun snapped but did not burst the cap." In his nervousness, he had put two caps on that were stuck together. "Just then a bullet struck a rotten rail and threw some of the splinters on me. My first thought was that I would be killed before I could shoot at all; I was still anxious to have one good battle, the fighting heretofore had not satisfied me." This continued as the fighting was taking place on the 81st Infantry's left. Once Campbell's men were able to hold off the enemy's charges, there continued to be the fire from sharpshooters who managed to find shelter behind trees and logs.[185]

Not only were sharpshooters a problem, but the Union line on the right of the 81st Illinois also gave way, thus allowing the Illinoisans to receive a deadly flanking fire. The gunfire was tremendous. According to James H. Orr, a private in the 81st Illinois Infantry, Company E, "Whiz! Whiz! Went the bullets around us. But we stood firm as a rock, and commenced pouring our volleys of musketry into them. This was too much, for they fell back; but in a few minutes they made a yelling charge on us, this time coming near enough to be seen, but quickly retreated." Flanking fire caused Orr to conclude, "Finally it was seen that we were in a condition to be badly flanked, and a retreat was ordered to prevent this." The right, coupled with the sharpshooting from the high ground to the left, made for a very precarious position for Campbell and his men. John Bartleson and five others found safety behind a "snag" as they watched the Southerners move upon the line they had just vacated. "Our business," according to Bartleson, "was now to shoot and shoot often, taking good sight and aim at men or near the bottom fence rails." The fighting began to take its toll on the 81st Illinois, as William Bellamy would be shot in the back, exclaiming, "Boys, I am shot...he was smiling with his last words." Others soon fell as Bartleson fired into the enemy, but when he turned back to see Bellamy, "his body had fallen forward and he was dead...I glanced to the left and Alfred Lingle was stretched out dead, without a struggle... The bark and rotten wood were raining constantly from the snag." Bartleson continued the fight. Even after his gun malfunctioned, he grabbed Bellamy's gun and continued fighting. Soon, however, "one of the boys just behind me was wounded in the neck. He had fallen with his head down hill. He called loudly, this was bad...Tom Hill was behind the log on my right in full sight. A bullet struck him square in the forehead." Of the six behind the snag, only John lived. To his right, the regiment had been involved in some "mixed hand to hand with the enemy" and had even captured a flag. Bartleson had started out with fifty cartridges; now he only had a few.[186]

The 81st Illinois Infantry held out under these circumstances until "every cartridge in the regiment had been expended, including those taken from the wounded and dead." Although Campbell had sent back his adjutant to procure ammunition, he never returned.[187] Now, the 81st Illinois was at its own crossroads. Campbell had no choice: "The men completely exhausted, out of ammunition, the enemy on the right, and a heavy enfilading fire on the left, that I ordered the regiment to fall back." The 81st Illinois moved back about three hundred yards, which also brought them near the artillery at Brice's Crossroads. Campbell was forced to relinquish command due to exhaustion, being overheated and also suffering from a previous illness. Command fell to Lieutenant Colonel Andrew W. Rogers.[188] As the battle continued, civilians were caught in the conflict. "The battle grew furious," recalled Martha Brice, "balls piercing the residence and tearing all of the tin gutters off the dwelling." The Brice home and the Bethany Church were turned into hospitals. Wounded and the dying "lay groaning about the premises." Mrs. Brice recalled, "An old lady had come over to spend the day,…She prayed this prayer all day: 'O Lord, take us all to heaven today, for we are all going to get killed.'"[189]

Meanwhile, as the men of the 81st Illinois were fighting for their lives, on their left stood the 95th Illinois Infantry. The men of the 95th Illinois had trouble from the start. Not long after they had fallen into line and the fighting had started, their beloved Colonel Humphrey was mortally wounded. Soon after receiving command, Captain William H. Stewart received a severe wound in both thighs and was carried from the field. Captain E.N. Bush took command and was soon after wounded. Command of the 95th Illinois now fell on Captain Schellenger. As the battle continued, men of the 95th Illinois began to fall "thick and fast from right to left of the regimental line." To add to the situation, ammunition was all but depleted, with none to arrive from the rear. Wales W. Wood, adjutant for the regiment, would later lament, "Neither the commanding officer of the troops, nor staff officers, appeared at the front, directing movements or bringing reenforcements to assist and strengthen the faltering Federal lines. They were not there to encourage or to share in the terrible fatalities of that eventful day." Finally, the 95th Illinois had to fall back due to being flanked on both ends of the regiment. It began to fall back, like many others, on Brice's Crossroads.[190]

The 108th and 113th Illinois Infantry Regiments suffered in the same way as the rest of the Second Brigade this day. Lieutenant Colonel Reuben L. Sidwell commanded the 108th Illinois and moved forward into line and along a ravine, but to his recollection, the infantry was not to "bring on an engagement." The skirmish line was sent out, and soon after this, "the enemy commenced an assault on us. Our left gave way first under the heavy fire…We all had to fall back then to prevent being surrounded." Rucker's men, along with Lyon, continued to apply pressure so that the long Union line continued to constrict itself farther and farther back to the crossroads.[191]

Lieutenant Colonel George Clarke of the 113th Illinois had just formed his men into the main Union line when he found the regiment to be under fire from the beginning. The position of the 113th Illinois was a very precarious place to be on the battlefield. It was also within this area that J.H. Mooney saw Sturgis on the field and recalled, "He was coming down toward us with his tall hat in his hand, swinging it as he came, and saying, give them hell boys—give them hell, he had hardly got the last hell out of him when the rebs threw a shell which passed through an oak tree nearly directly over his head, I thought some of the flying branches had struck him." Mooney continued, "He jumped up whirled on his heel & started back, at the same time calling for someone, and something about horses."[192]

Here the 113th Illinois regiment was situated on the Baldwyn road looking east, with its right anchored by the Union line, while to the left was a thick wooded area and the 95th Ohio Infantry somewhere in the mix. Already suffering from exhaustion, J.H. Mooney explained, "Rebel bullets commenced coming at us from both sides and front our men were ready to fall at every step from exhaustion, hunger, heat & thirst, our eyes half blind, the trees stumps & tombstones seemed to be moving round before us in a kind of foggy dance, our guns...not even having stopped to load, before driving us...into the middle of the enemys jaws." Within the dense foliage and den of battle, confusion reigned. Riley V. Beach of the 113th Illinois recalled that skirmishers were sent out and some rifle shots were fired, but the men were told to stop because they were shooting into their own men. However, the Union men to the right yelled out that the soldiers in question were in fact "Johnnys." Beach wrote, "I can see their gray jackets, someone says they are prisoners our boys have captured, and are marching to the rear, we soon found out I got sight of them; marching along a rail fence, trail arms four ranks deep, sooner than I can write it, bullets came from the front and right. We knew that we were flanked, at that time, if the rebs, pushed their advantage they could have captured the whole regt."[193]

The cemetery with a view across the Baldwyn road. Brice's Crossroads is about fifty feet to the right. *Courtesy of Emilee Bennett.*

"Order Soon Gave Way to Confusion and Confusion to Panic"

Earlier, McMillen had tried to bolster the line by sending one of the guns down the Baldwyn road about four hundred yards, but it, too, found itself in a bad place at the wrong time. It was now in the thick of the firestorm. Two of its horses were killed, and the piece was quickly taken along with two caissons. Beach and the rest of the 113th Illinois Infantry found themselves having to pull back their part of the line, thus leaving the 95th Ohio Infantry's right flank exposed. Lieutenant Colonel Jefferson Brumback was finding it difficult to keep the 95th Ohio together. They had already sent out two companies as skirmishers to cover the front and their weak left, and now the right was vulnerable as it set upon the Baldwyn road. Confederates hit the skirmishers, driving them back on the main line of the Ohioans. Brumback was caught on both flanks, forcing his men to retreat about forty to fifty yards. Yet again, the Confederates flanked their position, forcing the men to retire once again but this time about seventy-five yards within the dense woods and brush. Again, the right of the Ohioans was turned, and the regiment fell back to Brice's Crossroads. This time, they took their place behind a rail fence about fifty or more yards from the road.[194]

Clarke and the 113th Illinois Infantry also continued to fall back. With ammunition running out, sheer exhaustion setting in and a presumed belief that "we were being overpowered by superior numbers," the Illinoisans shot and retreated all the way back to Brice's Crossroads. Beach and his comrades fought back to a ravine and then finally back into the cemetery. During this back and forth running battle of the 113th Illinois, Beach heard the "rebel yell," stating, "I don't like it, it means a charge, we got it. The rebel yell sounds like a lot of Kilkenny cats while the Union cheer is full and round." The fight continued past the ravine and into the cemetery, but not before a good number of the regiment was captured. The fight in the cemetery became exceedingly difficult. There was no rest here for the living of the 113th Illinois. Beach could see all around him the struggle that was culminating at the crossroads just yards up the road. He recalled, "Splinters flying from the rail fence, chips from the tomb stones, our Adjutant, was killed here…and who helped to bury the dead; told me there were 54 buried here and the immediate vicinity."[195]

The battle had been raging around Brice's Crossroads for quite some time before Colonel C.R. Barteau and his 2nd Tennessee Cavalry entered the fight. Barteau, having only a part of his cavalry regiment, deployed his troopers and moved on the Union left rear. He realized that his forces would not pose a great threat to even a Union regiment, so he wisely followed the tactics his leader Forrest had turned to successfully in the past: deception.

The northeast area of Brice's Crossroads looking east toward the cemetery. The Baldwyn road is on the right of the cemetery. *Courtesy of Emilee Bennett.*

Barteau deployed his men under the cover of the woods and sent forward a thin yet lengthy line of skirmishers close up to the Union line. It was Barteau's plan to give the appearance of a massive attack without actually revealing his true numbers. This was achieved due to the abundance of undergrowth and small trees all along his line. Now Barteau's line was around three-quarters of a mile in length. Fortunately for Barteau, he had managed to approach the Federal position rather closely without being detected. He would later recall, "I deployed the regiment into a line nearly as long as that of the line of battle, and at once begun an attack by scattering shots. This led him to believe that my force was large, and to continue the impression I instructed my bugler to gallop along the whole line and at various points to sound the charge."[196]

Lieutenant Colonel Charles G. Eaton had placed five companies as skirmishers along the front and right of the 72nd Ohio Infantry in order to protect the far Union left. However, orders were received from Wilkin instructing the 72nd Ohio to move to the right of Mueller's battery, which was stationed by the log cabin on the ridge near the Tishomingo Creek and bridge. This move was being completed when heavy gunfire was heard between skirmishers of the 72nd Ohio and the Confederates. Once this

Log Cabin Ridge as seen from the north, with Tishomingo Creek to the right, out of the picture. Barteau's men of the 2nd Tennessee would have seen Log Cabin Ridge from this vantage point. *Courtesy of Emilee Bennett.*

occurred, the orders were countermanded, and the 72nd Ohio returned to its original position with its left almost at the foot of the hill. This time, however, Mueller had already withdrawn his artillery due to the fact that the 72nd Ohio had started its earlier move and would have left the guns unsupported. These guns were surely missed as the Ohioans continued their heavy skirmish fire. From the hill, Eaton could see "a heavy line of the enemy's skirmishers, which extended quite a distance beyond the left of my skirmish line, was seen advancing across the open field." Barteau's deception was having the effect he had hoped for. Although Eaton was able to fire a few volleys, which caused the 2nd Tennessee Cavalry to withdraw, it was only for a moment. Johnson's Alabamians were able to keep moving forward through the dense woods, while Barteau's men kept the 72nd Ohio busy skirmishing. Looking back, Barteau recalled, "I succeeded in reaching the Federal rear just as the fighting seemed heaviest in front." Barteau had managed to continue his charade of making his line appear longer than it was and making sure the bugler kept up the ruse of sounding the charge all along the line and "kept up as big a show as I could and a vigorous fire upon the Federals." He and his men were striking the Union left and rear at just the right time.[197]

McMillen's line was faltering. On the far Union right, the Confederate line was obstinate and continued to move forward. Hoge's line was feeling the stress of battle and was falling back, with regiments being flanked at every available opportunity. The battle was moving as Forrest wanted, but the Confederate right and especially news from the 2nd Tennessee Cavalry on the Union rear was sorely needed and expected. Finally, the news came from his trusted general. Buford had been busy keeping a careful watch on Johnson's and Lyon's forces as they continued to push forward, but he was also vigilant to keep watch for Barteau's Tennesseans. Buford had been able to ascertain from a cleared position on the right that the Union cavalry could be seen moving quite suddenly from Brice's Crossroads toward the Union rear. Once more, musketry could be distinguished to the Confederate right near Tishomingo Creek. Barteau and the 2nd Tennessee Cavalry had entered the fight.[198]

At this point in the fighting, all Union reserves had been committed to the battle. The major portion of Grierson's cavalry had been pulled out of line and, for the most part, also out of the battle. It was now later in the afternoon, around 4:00 p.m., as the battle continued to rage. Forrest's men had fought against incredible odds, but Forrest had used the environment to his army's advantage. The battle had reached its peak. Forrest had his troops exactly where he wanted them, and now he needed one final push against the Federal lines. As he rode along the rear of the Confederate line, he shouted out to the men, encouraging them and saying that the Union troops were giving way, that Barteau's men had reached the Union rear and one final effort would "sweep them from the field."[199]

Forrest hurried to Morton and his artillery, which were close up to the enemy and belching forth their leaden hail upon the hapless Federal soldiers. These guns were also in a much-exposed position, as was the nature for all on the battlefield this day. Forrest explained to Morton that he believed they had the Union army beaten and that although they clung to Brice's Crossroads, one more major push by the men would prove successful. The artillery was expected to play an active role. Forrest expected Morton to be ready with four artillery guns, which were to be double-shotted with canister, and to charge with the rest of the men when the bugle sounded for the charge. Morton's men were to hitch up the pieces, gallop to the front and get as close as possible to the Union line and fire upon them at close range. Forrest also rode to Buford and gave him instructions for the coming attack. However, when Buford heard what was expected of Morton and his guns, he warned Forrest of sending artillery so close to the enemy without support. Forrest

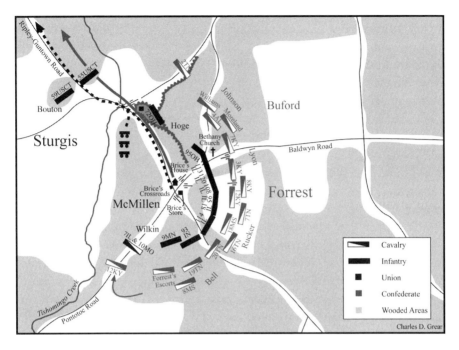

The assault on the Union infantry. *Courtesy of Dr. Charles Grear.*

merely stated, "Buford, all the Yankees in front of us cannot get to Morton's guns." Next, Forrest hurried over to Bell and Tyler concerning the battle plan. Tyler and his men, along with Captain Henry A. Gartrell's fifty men of Georgia and Forrest's escort made up of about eighty-five Tennesseans under the command of Captain John C. Jackson, were expected to assault along the Union right flank and continue to the rear of the Union line and engage any Unionists at pistol range between the right and the bridge at Tishomingo Creek.[200]

All was set for the final assault. Forrest would hit the front of the line hard while also smashing the Union flanks. Those on the far Confederate left would then break through to the rear and continue the attack. If the Union line collapsed in on itself, Forrest and his men would be victorious. If the Union line held, the casualty lists would not bode well for the Confederate army. Much was at stake, but Forrest was determined to keep the offensive. The plan was to aggressively hold the offensive while continuing to keep the Union commanders off balance. This had worked throughout the day so far.

When the charge was sounded, Forrest's men moved forward for the final push. The Union infantry had already been pushed back considerably, and for most, it was this final assault that caused the men in blue to fall back on Brice's Crossroads and beyond. Sturgis had been concerned about the situation on the left flank and rode down to investigate. He found the 72nd Ohio Infantry in good condition and also directed the management and protection of the wagons that had crossed Tishomingo Creek and to move them west across the creek. It was here that Sturgis began to realize that Confederate pressure on his right was "now becoming very great." He called on Grierson to help reinforce that area. Soon after, Sturgis received word that the cavalry that had been sent earlier to the right was giving way. More information came in detailing how the Southern troops were beginning to appear in force on the extreme Union left and rear. McMillen was also pleading for reinforcements in the center of the line.[201]

Morton and his artillerists were also ready when they heard the bugle sound. Four pieces of the artillery rushed forward along the narrow road. It must have surprised those of the Union line when they saw Morton's artillery rushing toward them. Morton was in front of them in close range of the center and right of the Federal line. Morton's artillery let loose double-shotted canister into the Northern ranks with telling effect. Together with Bell and Rucker's men, the worn-out Union line was completely broken. As the Union soldiers retreated back to Brice's Crossroads, Morton had the other guns moved up toward the new front, firing as they came.[202]

Sturgis realized that he had used what reinforcements he had on the field. However, he recalled that Bouton's Third Brigade Infantry might be able to save the army if they were not too far away from the battlefield. As Sturgis rode a short distance to where he expected to find the brigade, the nightmare for him and the Union army was realized: "The main line began to give way at various points. Order soon gave way to confusion and confusion to panic." McMillen was still fighting along the center of the line but needed reinforcements. Sturgis knew that any reinforcements he was to send would be too late, recalling, "The troops from all directions came crowding in like an avalanche from the battlefield, and I lost all possible control over them." He sent an aide to McMillen, admitting, "I was unable to render him any additional assistance, and that he must do all in his power with what he had to hold his position until I could form a line to protect his retreat." Along Brice's Crossroads, Hoge's Second Brigade continued to fall back. Beach of the 113th Illinois Infantry tried to fire on the enemy as he worked his way back to Brice's Crossroads but encountered another problem: "My gun got so foul I could not get the cartridge down; so I rammed it against a tree. It went so far in the thick bark I could not get it out." He further added, "I left it and picked up one, of many that were lying around." Beach soon found that the right of the line had "melted away." All was confusion now, and a man near Beach admitted, "I was in the first bull run battle, it was nothing to this." Beach caught sight of the crossroads area: "The near wheel horse, on a casion, was shot in the hip, when the bugle sounded retreat the others started, he fell the casion turned over, the other horses were cut loose and mounted by fleeing soldiers. It was now about 4:30 P.M. All organization was demoralized."[203]

If any Union position could have been considered in stable condition during the final Confederate assault, it would be toward the far Union right, which was held by the infantry regiments of the 9th Minnesota, the 93rd Indiana and, farther to their left, the 114th and 81st Illinois. But limited success on the right, for a time, didn't make up for the fact that when McMillen looked over his shoulder, he found what he called "considerable confusion." McMillen and his staff tried to rally and place the men in their original positions, but to no avail.[204]

McMillen desperately needed reinforcements, but now he had received Sturgis's reply and knew that without reinforcements, all was lost. He tried to extricate his men from Brice's Crossroads the best way he knew how. In desperation, he ordered the artillery to "open a rapid fire with grape and canister along the roads and through woods in our immediate front, and to maintain it until the infantry were well under way." He then added that he would develop a new line in order to keep the Confederates back from the crossroads until the artillerists could come away with their cannons. It was wishful thinking. Forrest's men were incredibly close to the artillery along Brice's Crossroads. Henry Hord of the Kentucky brigade remembered being about forty yards from the Union artillery during the final attack. As he and the others moved rapidly toward the prize guns, "I had pulled my cartridge box around on my hip…a ball struck one corner of it, spun me around and knocked me down, but I was not hurt. I jumped up and started again…The ball that struck my cartridge box jerked the belt up over the waist of the pants, and the first jump I made to go forward they dropped around my ankles…and threw me flat." Realizing that he was in the heat of battle, Hord "whirled over on my back and gave a vicious kick with both of my feet, and they went off my heels like a shot, striking square in the face one of our boys just rushing by…He thought it was a shell and could not understand why his head was still on."[205]

As the Union artillery was firing away, more and more of Forrest's men, such as W.D. Brown of the 8th Kentucky, gathered near the crossroads. Brown recalled years later passing "through the graveyard, and took shelter a few moments behind a church or storehouse while the Yanks were doing likewise…we pressed on to the road, capturing a caisson with team hitched to it, also four or five pieces of artillery." As Brown followed up the retreating Federals, "it developed into a glorious stampede…Soon we began to find guns, knapsacks, haversacks, hats, and quantities of private bric-a-brac." At one point in the crumbling of the Union line, the 3rd, 8th and 12th Kentucky were aligned to meet at Brice's Crossroads while the men of the 7th Kentucky, on the extreme right of the brigade, crashed into the Union left and bounded out of the woods between Brice's Crossroads and Tishomingo Creek, thus finding themselves on the Ripley-Guntown road. As Johnson continued to lead his Alabamians toward the Ripley-Guntown road, Major Hale led the 7th Kentuckians out of the woods and "wheeled to the right as soon as he reached the road. This placed him in advance of any of the remainder of Forrest's army and immediately behind the retreating and crushed Federals, who had been driven from their position around Brice's house."[206]

The 81st Illinois Infantry had fought hard this day, but it found itself, like the other Union regiments, falling back. "We continued to retreat," recalled Bartleson, "through a narrow piece of woods until we came to the cemetery and church at the crossroads. Lines were formed as best we could, ammunition was issued in a small amount, our artillery was stationed at the corner of the church, theirs was in front not far away." The landscape and properties were also feeling the effects of battle, as Bartleson found: "I turned to the church, not more than 40 or 50 feet away…Bullets were striking the church, chipping off the boards." Before he knew what was happening, Bartleson found the 81st Illinois moving down from the crossroads and toward the creek.[207]

As Sturgis's army continued to mass in the area of Brice's Crossroads, Tyler led Forrest's escort, reinforced by Gartrell's Georgians, who had continued to move along the Confederate far left flank. Now they bolted across the Pontotoc road, outflanking the under-strength 10th Missouri and the 7th Illinois Cavalry, and found themselves near Tishomingo Creek. While Tyler's men moved north, Barteau's 2nd Tennessee Cavalry was moving around from the south. The 72nd Ohio Infantry continued to play the major obstacle, keeping these troops and Tyler's from meeting at the bridge and thus cutting off the escape of Sturgis's army.[208] While more and more Union troops gathered all around Brice's Crossroads, it was becoming increasingly difficult to organize the men and make a stand on that line. As the artillery continued to fire, the wave of Confederate troops continued to cover the area. While confusion reigned here, it was important to keep the Ripley-Guntown road open to the retreating army. The 95th Ohio Infantry had been driven back to Brice's Crossroads, but now it had a new objective. Brumback drew his men across the Ripley-Guntown road and rallied behind a rail fence fifty to seventy-five yards away from, quite possibly, the Baldwyn road. This was to the left and rear of the Second Brigade and about a quarter of a mile from Brice's Crossroads. It was here that he was ordered "to hold as long as possible" so that the retreating army and artillery could make their escape. To the left of the 95th Ohio's new line was the 72nd Ohio in the position it had covered since skirmishing with Barteau's 2nd Tennessee. To the right of the 95th Ohio could be found the 93rd Indiana, with a detachment of the 10th Missouri Cavalry to their right. The problem with this line was that it could only hold as long as the Confederates were kept from charging down and flanking the men from the Ripley-Guntown road parallel with the new line. It was only a question of time.[209]

Meanwhile, back up the hill at Brice's Crossroads, soldiers in blue continued to stream down the Ripley-Guntown road and across Tishomingo Creek. As the Confederates continued to pound the mass of confusion with rifle and cannon fire, Company E of the 1st Illinois Light Artillery could be found in the middle of the crossroads fighting back. These men, under Captain John A. Fitch, had been ordered by Colonel McMillen to "hold the cross-roads at all hazards." Fitch suffered from what most of the Union army did this day, admitting, "I could not see the enemy, but judged from their firing that they were very near. I immediately gave them canister with both pieces as fast as I could load and fire." Fitch's men managed to hold their position until the Union regiments had passed. This also left Fitch with the sinking feeling that "so far as I could see I was left alone." The 1st Illinois Artillery remained in place and fired until it was fired on from its left and rear. Confederates fired on them from the Brices' garden, which was only about seventy-five feet from them. Miraculously, the Illinoisans quickly limbered their two remaining pieces and hurried off to the creek, where they were again fortunate to find that even though the Tishomingo Bridge was jammed, they were able to cross by traveling "forty rods below the bridge," where they connected with a road not far from the battlefield.[210]

Soon it was found that Forrest and his men controlled Brice's Crossroads. Lyon's Kentuckians were pushing toward Brice's house, and Morton's artillery arrived and unloaded on the Federals at close range. The two pieces of the 14th Indiana Battery, and possibly the ones that Sturgis told Grierson he would be responsible for, fell into the hands of Morton and his gunners. In no time, these guns were loaded and used on the Union soldiers streaming down the hill toward the bridge at Tishomingo Creek, as

Tishomingo Creek Bridge, from *Life of Lieutenant-General Nathan Bedford Forrest* by John Allan Wyeth. *Author's collection.*

well as on the Federals along Log Cabin Ridge. Bell, Rucker and their men gathered around the crossroads, along with Forrest. Tyler took the moment in and recalled, "It was but a few minutes when we all met at the crossroads. We were certainly a happy and enthusiastic band…Soon, however, we were in pursuit up the road towards Ripley." Before they could move on, the makeshift Union line parallel to the Ripley-Guntown road had to be cleared, and in the distance, Sturgis's Third Brigade could be seen moving toward the battlefield.[211]

Colonel Edward Bouton commanded the Third Brigade of Sturgis's expedition. His brigade was different from the others that were already in the fighting at Brice's Crossroads. Not only was it made up of troops of African descent, but many also were fighting this day in remembrance of what had happened at Fort Pillow. At Fort Pillow, it was believed that many

Log Cabin Ridge looking toward Brice's Crossroads. The crossroads are to the left center.
Courtesy of Emilee Bennett.

black soldiers were murdered after they had surrendered by troops under Forrest's command. This raised the ire of many people throughout the North regardless of their race. The Third Brigade troops now wore a badge stating, "Remember Fort Pillow." This was the day that they would have the chance to fight Forrest's men and possibly save the Union army.[212]

The Third Brigade had also double-quick marched for about three miles, but now the battlefield was coming into view. The men of the 55th U.S. Colored Troops saw the effect of the hot day on earlier infantrymen. Major Edgar M. Lowe would recall, "We passed hundreds if not thousands of men lying by the side of the road overcome with heat—some even dying from overexertion." As they continued down the road, cavalry could be seen falling back, and then the infantry and artillery. Bouton could tell from the sound of the battle that he needed to get his men to the front and quick. Two companies of the 55th USCT, under Captain Ewing, moved forward in what Bouton believed "seemed to be a gap in the First Brigade, near the right and rear of what seemed to be the left battalion." This would have been near the 72nd Ohio Infantry around and near Log Cabin Ridge. Soon after placing the two companies, seven more under Major Lowe were placed to the right and behind the first two original companies. McMillen had these men hold this position until the other troops that had been engaged in this area could retire. Then these men would follow from the rear. The men fought hard, but their numbers soon faltered due to loss, and they were "virtually crushed back by overwhelming numbers." In fact, Bouton would report, "Every commissioned officer of those two companies was killed or wounded in ten minutes." McMillen rode west toward Bouton, who was with the rest of his brigade in a good position to the right of the road. McMillen examined the terrain, looked at Bouton and inquired as to what the Third Brigade commander planned to do. Bouton clearly explained, "I told him I was going to put the battery in position on the ridge near the old house, put the Fifty-ninth in position on its right and the company of the Fifty-fifth on its left, bring the other companies of the Fifty-fifth to that place, and fight the enemy as long as I had a man left. It was like a breath of fresh air for McMillen, who had witnessed frustration and defeat throughout the day." In this last position, it was imperative that the Third Brigade hold the gray flood back in order to allow the retiring columns the opportunity to develop a new line to the rear. "That's right," fired back McMillen. "If you can hold this position until I can go to the rear and form on the next ridge you can save this entire command. It all depends on you now." That was the last order Bouton would receive this day. It would be 11:00 p.m. at Hatchie Bottom before he would see McMillen or Sturgis again.[213]

As Bouton's brigade continued its mission, what was left of the wagon train and artillery were moving down the road and away from the battlefield as quickly as possible. Meanwhile, back at Brice's Crossroads, the Confederates were massing and moving forward on the Union forces. Morton now had his artillery in place at the crossroads and had a commanding artillery fire that swept the distance of the Ripley-Guntown road and the log house ridge near the creek. "The battery boys working like double-geared lightning and firing double charges," recalled Hord. "The gun would jump off the ground at every discharge, but would hardly hit the earth before they would have another charge in it. They kept a constant stream of old iron going down the road after the Yankees, but they retired slowly, firing as they went." Even with Morton's guns thundering down upon them, the Federals managed to stand their ground. The view from Brice's Crossroads toward the west let the Confederates know that infantry reinforcements, along with artillery, were on their way to the battlefield. At this point in the fight, Barteau incorporated his own understanding of psychological warfare. In a loud voice, he called out, "Attention, battalion! Cease firing." When the firing stopped, he cried out, "Fix bayonets." Being cavalry, most if not all didn't carry a bayonet, but that was not the point. Barteau knew this as well as his troops did. However, they quickly understood that "he was talking for the benefit of the Yankees, who could hear him as plainly as we." The men moved forward to the sound of "Charge!" The Federals fired into them at close range and soon found themselves taken prisoner as they rushed to get away by wading across the creek. "We fired a volley in their backs as they came out on the opposite side." "Before reaching Tishomingo Creek," Forrest recalled, "the road was so blockaded with abandoned vehicles of every description that it was difficult to move the artillery forward." This didn't stop the victorious soldiers. Morton had the Tishomingo Bridge cleared for his artillery by throwing the wagons, along with dead men and horses, into the creek below. The Confederate infantrymen, who were soaked from jumping into the creek after the bluecoats, continued the relentless surge of the gray tide.[214]

The 3rd Iowa Cavalry had made it across the Tishomingo Creek earlier, but not the 4th Iowa Cavalry. Now, they found themselves in a precarious position. The bridge was blocked due to broken-down teams, and the banks of the Tishomingo were too steep, making it impossible to get the horses across. Furthermore, Union soldiers continued to make their way down from Brice's Crossroads, with Forrest's men following in great haste while

Johnson's Alabamians came through the woods to the east and Barteau's 2nd Tennesseans continued their push around Log Cabin Ridge from the northeast. Even worse was the fact that Morton's artillery was playing upon the 4th Iowa's position, firing grape and canister in their direction. Major Pierce acted quickly. He dismounted his men and had them scramble up the log house ridge. "We held the entire force of the enemy from this point for more than thirty minutes." The bridge was cleared, and every horse crossed over the creek. McMillen rode along the new and final line and directed the officers to hold the line until the troops and artillery were safely across. Once this had been completed, they were to fall back "across the creek with as little confusion as possible." The Iowans kept up the fire, thus also allowing a number of the infantry to pass before the Iowans could be surrounded. Once across the creek, the men mounted their horses and joined the 3rd Iowa Cavalry once again. The 4th Iowa was considered the last organized Union regiment to leave the battlefield.[215]

Chapter 7

"If Mr. Forrest Will Let Me Alone
I Will Let Him Alone"

It was a dismal march west from the battlefield for the defeated Union army. Eaton, with his 72ⁿᵈ Ohio Infantry, moved along the right side of the road, watching as the wagons made their way toward Ripley. They had barely escaped capture near Log Cabin Ridge, and now Grierson rode up with a suggestion. The 72ⁿᵈ Ohio was to take a position behind a rail fence about a half mile from the battlefield in order to safeguard the wagon train. This Eaton and his Ohioans did until the last wagon past. After the close fight they had just endured, this only added to the stress. All was successful. However, as if to add insult to injury, as the evening came on, Eaton found that the teamsters within the middle of the train "began to destroy their wagons by setting them on fire, thus blockading the road so that all the wagons in the rear of those destroyed had to be abandoned." After marching at the double-quick in a hot sun and fighting a losing battle, Eaton's men completed another march of eight miles from the battlefield before finally getting a short rest until orders came from Sturgis to keep moving. Now twelve miles out and dead tired, they came to a halt only to move out again under orders to march to Ripley. Six miles south of Ripley, Eaton saw Sturgis and McMillen and was ordered to continue on, "which I did, arriving there at 5 o'clock the following morning, having in twenty-three hours marched a distance of thirty-eight miles, and engaged the enemy two hours." The same situation was true for many a soldier in Sturgis's army this day.[216]

Captain Ewing, along with his two companies of the 55ᵗʰ USCT, rejoined the other seven companies that were brought into the fight near

Log Cabin Ridge. Together, they covered the Tishomingo bottomlands, while the other Federal soldiers and what was left of the wagon train made their escape toward Ripley. It was around this time that Major Lowe received a severe wound to his arm, whereupon command was transferred to Captain A.T. Reeve. Reeve and his regiment moved up about a quarter of a mile toward the hill Bouton had prepared as the Third Brigade's fallback point. Here they joined the 59th USCT. The 55th USCT formed on the left of the 59th USCT, with the right of the 55th USCT resting on the road. Bouton developed his line, "thus formed being somewhat in the form of a scroll, conforming to the ridge on which it was formed." Captain C.A. Lamberg's battery was in position near the old house also known as the Ames residence. The battery threw shells fused at two and a half to three seconds toward the oncoming Confederate wave, which was just in the woods behind the retreating Union troops. Forrest's men didn't let up but came on in force. Lamberg's battery depressed their artillery and let loose a curtain of canister that covered the open ground, but to no avail. Confederates continued swarming toward them. The Third Brigade Infantry poured a heavy fire into the gray line. This time, Forrest's men were stopped in their tracks. However, they regrouped, and again the gray tide continued forward. The Third Brigade found their right "forced back and flanked," causing the whole line to fall back. This line held out for about thirty minutes or more until the Confederates came in a heavy rush on their left flank. The colored troops were now in retreat at the double-quick. The officers and men would stop and fight for a while until flanked, and then the chase was on again. Many were overcome by exhaustion.[217]

Captain Lamberg's artillery was put in position, and the men rallied around this new makeshift line, yet they were hit with a furious assault from the left flank. Lamberg could not see the enemy and almost lost his guns in this attack but managed to limber up and move out quickly to the rear. The men made their way back upon the road only to find it strewn with wagons in all types of disorganization. Some of these wagons were without teams, while others were on fire. Retreating still farther, the colored troops found themselves among the white Union infantry who had stopped and formed along the road near a white house. The men of the 59th USCT found themselves also fighting, being flanked and involved in a running gun battle through the fields and deep woods until they also reached the White House Ridge area. It was also here at White House Ridge that Sturgis and McMillen examined the last line of defense before moving in the direction of Hatchie Bottom.[218]

It was possible that the stress of the day had finally unnerved Sturgis. While on the White House Ridge line, Captain Egbert O. Mallory of the 114th Illinois Infantry was near Sturgis and reported, "I saw general Sturgis and Colonel McMillen with a bottle of whisky about sundown on that day where we formed our last line…I saw Colonel McMillen pass the bottle to General Sturgis and saw him [General S.] take a drink." Sturgis did not stay long on the ridge but continued on his way toward Hatchie Bottom. It was another story for the colored troops who had just arrived on the line. Ammunition for the colored troops was sorely needed. They found what they needed in this position and smashed open the boxes, taking all they could to fill their cartridge boxes, and then formed behind the line of infantry. Sadly, Captain Reeve recalled, "I saw nothing that acted very much like an organization, but it looked like a regular stampede." Forrest's men continued their assaults, causing the 59th USCT to retreat about five hundred yards to a ridge with a cotton gin and gin house. Here, Lieutenant Colonel Robert Cowden finally relinquished command of the 59th USCT after receiving a severe hip wound earlier in the day. Just two hundred yards in the rear of the 59th USCT, Cowden came upon Wilkin, who was trying to form a line. The 59th USCT would join Wilkin's makeshift line.[219]

It wasn't in Forrest's nature to let the enemy leave the battlefield to lick their wounds. It wasn't any different after the Battle of Brice's Crossroads. Forrest had his men immediately follow up on the fighting by chasing after the defeated Sturgis and his wounded expedition. Forrest wanted a complete victory with all the spoils of war, and since he followed the enemy so closely, his men were able to continue capturing men and material. There was still enough sunlight left in the day to continue harassing the defeated Union army. Forrest realized that he needed fresh men for the fight and had those who had served as horse holders during the fighting take up the chase. He would not let up on Sturgis and his Union army, later writing, "He [Sturgis] attempted the destruction of his wagons, loaded with ammunition and bacon, but so closely was he pursued that many of them were saved without injury, although the road was lighted for some distance." At one point during the follow-up of Sturgis's army, word came back to Forrest that the Union soldiers were, in fact, burning their wagons. At that, Forrest ordered his men to "Move up in front!" This communication between the front and Forrest continued to miscue as the same question and answer was exchanged several times. Finally, Forrest made his way to the front and exclaimed, "Don't you see the d__d Yanks are burning my wagons? Get off your horses and throw the burning beds off!" In no time, Forrest's men were dismounted, and off came the burning beds. However, one lieutenant did not help. When Forrest yelled out to ask him why he wasn't helping, the answer Forrest received was that the man was an officer. In characteristic fashion, "Forrest made at him with his sabre drawn, 'I'll officer you,' and no acrobat ever was quicker in a movement than our brave lieutenant in getting to the ground; and a full hand he made in upsetting the wagon beds." Forrest and his men did what they could to put out the fires and kept up the chase. There was still sunlight left, and the ever-vigilant Forrest sent out a detachment to watch Sturgis's forces. Victory and rest would eventually come to Forrest's men.[220]

Sturgis watched as all was confusion running from the battlefield. He found Winslow leading his cavalry brigade away from the fight and, according to Sturgis, "never halted until he had reached Stubbs', ten miles in rear…This was the greater pity, as his brigade was nearly, if not entirely, intact, and might have offered considerable resistance to the advancing foe." Waring's first brigade of cavalry, along with Grierson, also moved out. According to Grierson, they moved with orders from Sturgis to put his First Brigade "in advance of the retreating forces, with instructions to check the retreat and open the road to the rear." Grierson and the First Brigade also headed for Stubb's plantation, which was a good ten miles from the battlefield. As evening approached, Grierson and his staff traveled to Stubb's plantation, where they found Winslow's brigade. Winslow had been ordered by Sturgis to "proceed to Ripley…was permitted to stop at Stubb's plantation…stating to Colonel Winslow that his artillery and train 'had already gone to Hell.'" Grierson also stated that Sturgis had ordered Waring's brigade "rapidly to Ripley." Grierson and his cavalry were able to help shield those soldiers heading back from that locale. However, Wilkin's infantry, still back along a ridge with a white house not far from the battlefield, helped hold a line fighting any oncoming Confederates as best they could with what they had.[221]

As the sound of battle was waning around Brice's Crossroads and Tishomingo Creek, Samuel Agnew was growing ever anxious. "It became evident," according to Agnew, "about 5 o'clock that the firing was nearer, that the Federals were manifestly falling back and that Forrest was pressing them in this direction." Around 6:00 p.m., Agnew realized, "To my surprise shells began to fall in the woods where we were hidden…as the shells passed over my head whizzing and spluttering, I couldn't help dodging." Realizing he was no longer in a safe place, Agnew retreated with his brother, knowing that "the battle was evidently raging there. I was anxious in reference to the dear ones at home." He took the livestock two miles away and hid them, safe from capture. Then they went to Reverend J.L. Young's home. Agnew started back to his home early the next morning, being ever cautions, as he didn't know which side—Union or Confederate—possessed the house and the rest of the ridge area.[222]

Wilkin had his hands full back at the Agnew house. The home was situated on a ridge near the Ripley road and between Dry Creek and Little Dry Creek. Its proximity to Brice's Crossroads and being so near the Ripley-Guntown road made it an easy choice for the broken Union army to fall back upon. Having felt the stress of finding himself "left alone" when the brigades made their escape as he and his men held a line at Tishomingo Creek, Wilkin was fighting alone yet again. The various troops that were supposed to be on his flanks during the retreat had moved out and left his flanks unsupported and volatile to Confederate attack. This caused Wilkin's men to keep firing while also retreating. Once on White House Ridge with the two-story Agnew home nearby, a new line had developed that included the infantry regiments of the 93rd Indiana, 81st Illinois, 72nd Ohio, 95th Ohio, 114th Illinois and 9th Minnesota. While these hardened veterans made a good line, there were two acute problems. First, the 114th Illinois, like so many other regiments at this time, found itself either low on or out of ammunition. A staff officer was sent

The Samuel Agnew family and their home on White House Ridge in 1896. Samuel Agnew is seated at the lower right of the picture. *Courtesy of Sam Agnew, Private Collection.*

to bring up a supply, "but finding no means of transportation he brought back one box on his horse." The second problem was that many of these regiments took the road back to Ripley when they realized that the Third Brigade had bought them time to retreat. This left the 55th USCT on the left rear of the line when it happened upon the line later in the afternoon. To its front was the 59th USCT, with their left anchored on the 9th Minnesota, and on the far left could be found the 114th Illinois. These last two regiments were on the right of the Ripley road when looking to the northwest. The line consisted of the 59th USCT to the right, with the 9th Minnesota to the center and the 114th Illinois to the left when looking toward the Confederate advance.[223] The Confederates were coming up as the sun was sinking in the western sky. It was in this position on White House Ridge that King of the 114th Illinois saw Sturgis, along with McMillen and Wilkin. According to King, "McMillen told Wilkin to hold the rear until it got dusk, and he would go ahead and reorganize and form a line on a chosen position to protect us." This next line would take Wilkin and his men back to Hatchie Bottom.[224]

Forrest and his men had been through a lot this day, but he understood that their work was not over yet. The men moved along the Ripley road toward White House Ridge and the Agnew house. Forrest was with Morton and his artillery as they moved down the road about two miles from the battlefield and across Dry Creek. Here, Morton unlimbered the artillery, which included two guns each from Morton's and Rice's batteries, along a wooded ridge near a ravine. Whereupon, Union skirmishers continued their rifle fire on the Confederate artillery from White House Ridge just across this ravine. Morton and Rice were keeping up a "rapid fire" against this Union line when Forrest and an orderly rode up. Forrest dismounted and walked over near the artillery. Captain Morton saw the general and stated, "General you had better get a little lower down the hill." Catching himself, Morton expected Forrest to remind the artillerist that it was none of his business as to where the general should go and offered up an apology: "Excuse me, General, I don't purpose to say where you should go." Surprisingly, "Genl Forrest walked a short distance down the hill for a seat." It was getting more serious around the artillery as the enemy bullets "were cutting the leaves from the trees," recalled Bell. "The cannoniers were almost exhausted and famished and drank the black powder water out of the sponge buckets." Bell believed that the artillery could limber up and move out much more quickly than the cavalry, as cavalry had to remount and form into a cavalry regiment. This might have given Forrest something to think about while sitting below the hill listening to the roar of the cannons. After Forrest had

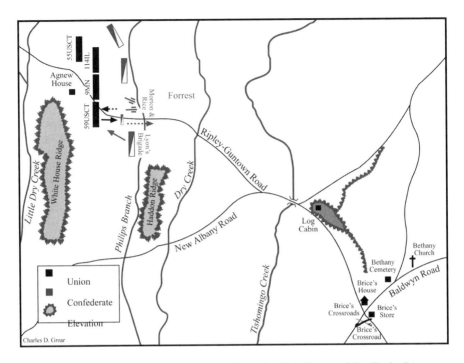

The last defensive line of the Union army on June 10, 1864. *Courtesy of Dr. Charles Grear.*

sat for about twenty minutes resting, he called Morton down to meet with him as he sat at the root of a tree. Forrest explained, "Captain, you see my column coming up that road? I am going to take command of that column and charge across this open field and strike them on that flank. Pointing to the right flank of the federals. When you hear Gause sound the bugle for the charge, you take your artillery and charge down that road and give them hell right over there where I am going to double them up." Rice had heard the conversation and went to Morton, questioning, "Do you think Gen. Forrest means for us to charge them without support?" Captain Morton laughingly remarked, "Captain you hear the orders, be ready to move."[225]

Forrest did make the charge across the field, attracting the attention of Wilkin's men. As these men fired on Forrest and his troops, Morton and Rice charged forward about 150 yards from the Union line, unlimbered and "opened a rapid fire with double shotted canisters." As the Federals fired at Forrest, the Confederate artillery continued to fire into the blue line. It would be remembered that "the fire of the canister shot caused great havoc among the troops and it was found that there were more dead men

The Old Ripley road near White House Ridge and the Agnew home. *Courtesy of Emilee Bennett.*

The Ripley road looking toward the Union line. The Samuel Agnew home was behind this line and would have been to the right in this picture. *Courtesy of Emilee Bennett.*

in that place than any other point on the battlefield." This was also the area in which the 114th Illinois and the 59th USCT held the line while the 9th Minnesota would have possibly been to Morton's right and center. Marsh of the 9th Minnesota would recall the fighting to be fierce and that many Confederates were killed, but he also admitted that they "held them in check until again ordered to retire, when we fell back into the road in good order, fighting every step, and again brought up the rear."[226]

Before Marsh's men and the rest of the line retired, Morton's artillery moved forward up the road quickly until it was at the edge of a wooded ridge. Lieutenant Brown's section of artillery was placed to the right of the road. This position would prove to be one of the more fatal of the day for the artillery, for at this point the Union line made a stand that staggered Morton's guns. It was here that the 59th USCT charged and drove the Confederates back while using their bayonets and guns as clubs. These men pushed back the gray line while carpeting the area with the dead. Some believed that the colored troops fought so passionately because of the incident at Fort Pillow, stating, "The enemy charged through the woods from their position so close that the members of the artillery could hear the officers exalt their men to stand firm, and 'Remember Fort Pillow.'"

They made it within fifty to seventy-five yards of the Confederate guns and caused them to be in danger of being captured. One man of the artillery was killed, while several others were wounded. The charge of Morton's artillery had an impact on Wilkin, who would write, "The enemy poured into the fields in great force when we kept up a fire for about twenty minutes, causing great slaughter & driving them back. They brought up their artillery and shelled us. I ordered the command to retire, which they did in good order, the enemy pursuing us no further. It was so dark." During the fighting around the artillery, a Kentucky regiment under Lyon moved toward the right of the artillery in a flanking movement and, raising the Rebel yell, was able to attack and beat back the colored troops. By this time, the Union line was giving way, and Morton was able to move his artillery up to Dr. Agnew's house. Here could also be found many wagons left by Sturgis and the retreating Federals. Although the Federal forces fell back, they continued to give ground grudgingly. The sun was finally setting as the Union troops made their way toward Hatchie Bottom.[227]

Now with darkness upon them, Forrest allowed his men to rest, but not before sending out some of his men in advance in order to follow the enemy slowly but carefully. The others would eat and rest.[228] Sturgis, however, would not have a restful night. The Battle of Brice's Crossroads had finally ended. Although the battle was over, the long road back to Memphis for Sturgis and his soldiers was to become a nightmare few, if any, would ever forget.

After leaving the area of the Agnew home on White House Ridge, Wilkin moved his men northwest along the Ripley road around 8:30 p.m. Soon, they found themselves fighting a new battle, but this time it was with the environment. The soldiers had traveled about four miles when they encountered more wagons and artillery that had bogged down in Hatchie Bottom. The deep mud of Hatchie Bottom proved difficult for all the retreating soldiers, regardless of whether they were an organized group or mob. Dr. L. Dyer, surgeon in chief to the infantry and artillery, was with one of the hospitals on the field. His frustration built when he found his organization constantly moving in retreat with the rest of the army due to Forrest's men continuing to press them. He recalled "lifting the poor mangled fellows into the ambulances once more the drivers were directed to fall into the retreating column…The road was not wide enough. It was filled up to overflowing from fence to fence, with wagons, ambulances, artillery, horsemen and footmen—everybody trying to get ahead of everybody else!" Finally, after reaching the area around Hatchie Bottom, it was found that a caisson had "stuck fast in the mud" and the wagon train with most of Sturgis's army equipment and supplies would have to be left behind. This also included the wounded. The officer in charge of the ambulance train and the surgeons did all they could to get the ambulance wagon and the wounded out and to safety, but it was futile. In the end, they exhausted themselves and were finally compelled to leave all. When this was decided, Dr. Dyer wrote, "There in the wilderness, in the darkness and gloom of midnight, our wounded companions were taken out, and gently laid upon the bosom of mother earth—the precious trust left to the tender mercies of the advancing foe!" In a last hopeful act, Dyer took the time to prepare "a respectful note to the surgeons of the Confederate army, soliciting their kind offices in behalf of such of our wounded men, as might, by the fortunes of war, fall into their hands; and I have learned with much satisfaction, that these men received the kindest treatment."[229]

Captain Lee of the 7th Wisconsin Battery, and in charge of the artillery of the cavalry division, had managed to get his artillery out of the tangled mob around Brice's Crossroads. However, he could not escape the clutches of Hatchie Bottom. He was able to get one gun and three limbers through the muck, but the others were another matter. The rest of his artillery had to be left behind due to the "abandoned ambulances, drowned and dying horses and mules, and the depth of the mud." He and the men worked for four and a half hours trying to get the artillery through but finally gave up. Before he abandoned them, "I spiked the other piece, dismounted it, and threw it into a sink-hole, where it went down about eight feet. I cut down all the carriages, and threw all the ammunition in the mud that I could not bring away." The few that Lee was able to save would only be destroyed and abandoned later in the retreat.[230]

It was around midnight when Wilkin finally realized that the wagons were "irretrievably stuck." The only thing to do now was to unhitch the animals and move on. Although it was dark, Wilkin remembered, "With difficulty we got through the swamp. Cannon wagons & ambulances were in the mud. Horses were floundering about & men were rushing past each other in the wildest confusion. The darkness of the night was hideous." While this was more than enough for the officers and common soldiers to bear, the early morning also brought the hoof beats of Confederate horses upon the hapless Federal army. These horsemen came at different times in small and large parties and harassed Sturgis's men almost all the way to Memphis.[231]

It was around 11:00 p.m. on June 10, when Colonel Bouton came upon Sturgis and McMillen as they were attempting to cross Hatchie Bottom.

He also saw before him the long line of wagons that were abandoned and artillery that had been spiked and left in the road. Bewildered at the sight, Bouton pleaded with Sturgis, "General, for God's sake don't let us give up so." Sturgis, lost in the defeat of the day, inquired, "What can we do?" Thinking quickly, the colonel explained, "Give me the ammunition that the white troops were throwing away in the mud and I would hold the enemy in check until we could get those ambulances, wagons, and artillery all over that bottom and save them." Furthermore, Bouton requested, "Give me one of those white regiments to help lift the wagons and artillery over, that I would stake my life that I would save the whole of them." Sturgis had a colonel ready and willing to fight. He could have been the man to help stop the rear guard raids on the retreating army and save the wounded along with the wagons and bring them all back to Memphis. Saving some of the wagons and artillery associated with the expedition would surely be better than just a half-starved, defeated partial army. Instead, Sturgis snapped back at the colonel, "For God's sake, if Mr. Forrest will let me alone I will let him alone. You have done all you could and more than we expected of you, and now all you can do is to save yourselves."[232] Many of the Union soldiers dropped and tried to get some rest; however, the men of the 59th USCT continued their retreat and, worse, without ammunition. They marched, picking up discarded cartridges as they went, until reaching Ripley early the next morning.[233]

The fight had gone out of Samuel D. Sturgis. He had come a long way from his early days at West Point and his first tests among the Indian fighting and buffalo stampedes. He commanded an army of battle-hardened veterans and lost miserably. All he had to show to Washburn and Sherman was a partial, emaciated army. According to J.B. Russell, the chief ordnance officer, Forrest's command had captured sixteen artillery pieces, numerous carriages, caissons and limbers and an abundance of ammunition for artillery and small arms. Most of Sturgis's wagons had been captured, along with horses, mules and various accouterments that were needed by Forrest's command. These items would, most likely, play a part in future Confederate exploits. By June 13, most of Forrest's men had given up the chase; however, Confederate reports revealed that a staggering 1,618 men had been captured from Sturgis's Federal army.[234] Sturgis's only hope was to make it safely back to Memphis. For Sturgis, however, the fight would not end in Memphis. Sherman refused to believe Sturgis's expedition had battled 15,000 to 20,000 Confederates, calling it "nonsense." Sherman expected the matter to be "critically investigated." Rumors had also reached

Sherman's ears that Sturgis might have been drunk during the battle. To this, Sherman wrote McPherson about having the history of the defeat of Sturgis by Forrest investigated, "especially whether it, in any measure, resulted from General Sturgis being in liquor." Sherman would later write to the adjutant general of Sturgis's plight, even going as far as to make excuses for him, stating, "He was dealing with a bold and daring foe, on fresh horses, familiar with the roads and by-paths." Maybe it was Sherman's way of helping out a West Pointer like himself. In the end, Sturgis would get his day in the court of the Board of Investigations. Sturgis would not be dismissed from the service; however, his days of commanding an army in the field during the Civil War were over. As the evening turned to morning, the only thing left for Sturgis to celebrate was his forty-second birthday—a birthday he would never forget.[235]

The men of Sturgis's army were also focused on getting back to Memphis safely. For some, it would take days due to the fact that Forrest and his Confederate cavalry were relentless in their follow-up to gather all they could in the way of wagons, artillery and prisoners. Forrest and his men continuously kept the Union soldiers off balance. "I was 3 days and nights without a bite to eat once captured, got away, and lay in my tent in Fort Pickering 4 or 5 weeks from prostration," recalled an unfortunate officer from the 55th USCT. Forrest and his men attacked the Union rear at Ripley on June 11 and kept the raid going well toward Memphis. Many Union soldiers would hide in the woods and even swamps along the way, only to be captured and made to walk back to Brice's Crossroads. One soldier of the 55th USCT remembered the ordeal in retreating back to Memphis: "I soon gave out and had to take the bushes. Lieut. Gulliver…and myself crawled in to a swamp where we lay until pretty nearly dark." One soldier admitted to his wife, "Vicksburg was play compared with this fight. Some officers who were in the Battle of Shiloh, say this was far worse for the time it lasted…They followed us 80 miles like wolves. It makes me sad to see the regiment so small, and I feel as if I had been to a great funeral." Many of the captives were sent to Andersonville Prison, where a number of them died. Those who lived never forgot Brice's Crossroads, and few forgave Sturgis. J.C. Allen of the 9th Minnesota Infantry, Company A, believed, "We lost from our regiment at Guntown and the three following days, about five hundred men, most of whom went to Andersonville and never returned." It was also a common belief felt by many in Sturgis's expedition that "Sturgis was a traitor, and it is certain that a man with any brains could have conducted a battle better than he did."[236]

Regardless, those who did make it back to Memphis or made it through Andersonville usually despised Sturgis. "This fight showed that Sturgis," according to Colonel D.W.C. Thomas of the 93rd Indiana Infantry, "was totally unfit to command, his actions proved cowardice and his military dispositions were evidence of a regular *sell-out* to Forrest."[237] Much of the arguing over Sturgis's lack of generalship and character would take place years after the war. But at this point, just after the battle, being captured and sent to Andersonville for some and reaching Memphis before getting captured by Forrest for others was the most important situation to focus on.[238]

Back at Brice's Crossroads, the debris of battle could be seen all across the fields, in the cemetery and on the roads. One Union soldier who passed over the battlefield saw "the most sickening sights of unburied and half-buried soldiers that I ever saw. In many instances the hogs were rooting our boys from the shallow graves in which they had been buried." One Union soldier who was captured and taken to Guntown in late June, only weeks after the battle, found that "in going to Guntown we passed over the same road our army had fought and retreated, the entire route affording a scene and a stench I have no desire to remember." Concerning the colored troops, "I saw those colored boys start in, fight, and die; as I passed along the road I saw their unburied bodies all the way from Ripley to the road on the hill, bloated and bursting."[239] Samuel A. Agnew came out of the fields from hiding once he believed the fighting had subsided. As he examined the aftermath of battle, he found that Mr. Brice's home was now serving as a hospital for the wounded Confederate soldiers. "Southern boys lay on pallets there, and some died there." Mrs. Brice was there helping with the wounded and dying. The Bethany church also served as a hospital for the Union wounded: "Many a Federal soldier lay wounded on benches on which worshippers had been wont to sit in days when peace reigned in the land." He also found that a bullet had passed through the pulpit, while the monument and tombstones in the nearby cemetery showed the wear of war with bullet imprints.[240]

Agnew traveled toward his house, the white house on the ridge that had seen the last of the fighting that eventful day. "The public road in both directions was lined with wagons as far as could be seen. As I came home," recalled Agnew, "for more than half a mile, I saw hundreds of shoes and articles of every description which had been thrown away by the Yankees in their retreat. The road was filled with soldiers passing to and fro. When I saw these things I knew that Forrest had gained a great and complete victory." Agnew finally reached his house to find that it "was a wreck." He found his family safe and that the ladies of the family were on the back piazza. "They were laughing and talking but under their mirth I could see a sadness concealed." Agnew found that all their food was taken and, when walking through the rooms of the house, "found everything turned upside down and that many things had been taken from us. Dead and wounded men were lying in the house, upstairs and downstairs. Bullets had penetrated the walls of the house in various places."[241] Agnew's land would also serve as a burial ground for some. "A man named King of Rice's battery, is buried a few hundred yards below my residence; the little mound which marks his grave can be seen on the roadside." He recalled that A.J. Smith "is not far away but the exact spot cannot be pointed out."[242] The Agnew family, the Brices and the rest of the community felt the cruelties of war that didn't heal for a long time.

Nathan Bedford Forrest and his cavalry managed to achieve what many thought impossible. At Brice's Crossroads, a largely outnumbered Confederate force attacked and defeated a Union army that was about twice the size of its opponent. Forrest reported that his available force during this fight stood at only 3,500 men, while Sturgis rounded off his numbers to be about 8,000.[243] What Forrest and his men achieved at Brice's Crossroads made him a legend to many people of Mississippi, the western theater and the rest of the Southern Confederacy. Forrest was able to capitalize on much of his quickly laid battle plan partly due to the fact that Sturgis allowed himself to be drawn into the trap. Had Sturgis recalled Grierson from Brice's Crossroads to another point closer to his infantry along one of the ridges of his own choosing, he might have been able to contain the situation. However, by fighting Forrest in and around Brice's Crossroads, Sturgis would have to consider the negative effects the environment would have on his position and troops. What Forrest had that Sturgis increasingly needed was information. Forrest knew how many troops Sturgis had, while Sturgis was always kept guessing about the number of the enemy. To pull back from Brice's Crossroads would have given Sturgis more time to plan how he was going to fight and where he would fight and to possibly fight on his own terms. Sturgis's decisions depended on leadership. Forrest had the plan, timing, concealment, aggressiveness and leadership needed to make the victory happen. Another important reason for Forrest's victory can be seen in the way he used his men. Forrest had cavalry that could ride but could also dismount and fight like infantry. Either way, his men were mobile and able to adapt quickly to mounted and dismounted operations. Forrest was also allowed to fight on the ground of his choosing regardless of whether Grierson commanded Brice's Crossroads or not. In other words, as long as the fight took place relatively in that area, Forrest could still find ways to conceal his men. Forrest understood the area and used the environment to conceal his numbers to work to his advantage. For years to come, men in Sturgis's expedition believed that Forrest had at least the same amount of men as they did, if not more.[244]

Forrest's win at Brice's Crossroads did not come without a price. Confederate casualties for this victory were hard to replace. S.D. Lee would write the authorities in Richmond of Forrest's exploits, announcing that Forrest had, "gained a complete victory, capturing many prisoners and wagon train." Yet in the end, Lee wrote, "our loss quite severe." When examining the returns for both armies in killed and wounded, it can be found that those killed or wounded of the Union army were 617 total, while the Confederate army lost 492. Considering that Forrest's command was much smaller to begin with, the loss was, as Lee mentioned, "quite severe." The largest difference in this battle was the number of Union soldiers taken as prisoners. Making up for lost men would always be a difficulty for the Confederacy. Soon after the dust settled at Brice's Crossroads, Forrest would fight again, but this time as a subordinate on the field of battle to S.D. Lee. Tupelo was the battlefield, and Lee and Forrest's men would suffer defeat. Both of these battles, a victory and a defeat, drained Confederate manpower that was slowly strangling the Confederacy. Regardless, Forrest would continue to lead his men through the thickest of the fighting, continue to be victorious on many occasions until the war would draw to a close and keep Sherman tense and frustrated until Atlanta had fallen.[245]

It is true that Brice's Crossroads was a spectacular victory for the Southern Confederacy in the West, and it buoyed the spirits of the people of north Mississippi for a time; however, it is important to consider the bigger picture of the war. Sherman's main objective was to keep Forrest off his supply lines and possibly capture or kill Forrest while Sherman continued to focus on taking Atlanta and defeating Joseph E. Johnston's army. When Washburn, McPherson and Sherman received the news of Forrest's victory at Brice's Crossroads, it only intensified the war in the region in which Forrest operated. As early as June 13, Sherman wrote Washburn back in Memphis with a new plan to send out A.J. Smith's command for a new expedition to stop Forrest, reminding Washburn, "I don't see what Forrest can have except his cavalry, and the militia… They should be met and defeated at any and all cost." Sherman also wrote to the secretary of war, Edwin M. Stanton, his plan: "To send as large a force again as he can get on Forrest's trail, and harass him and the country through which he passes…We must destroy him if possible." To McPherson, Sherman spelled out his plan completely, in which a large force was to be sent out to pursue Forrest and devastate the land that Forrest was in. Sherman decided to bring forward the hard hand of war, stating, "Make him and the people of Tennessee and Mississippi realize that, although a bold, daring, and successful leader, he will bring ruin and misery on any country where he may pause or terry. If we do not punish Forrest and the people now, the whole effect of our past conquests will be lost." Sherman seemed desperate to keep Forrest off his supply line, so much so that he pledged his influence with President Lincoln to help make General Mower a major general if Mower could defeat Forrest. By June 22, Washburn had written Sherman to let him know that A.J. Smith was on his way with nine thousand infantry and three thousand cavalry, along with four batteries of artillery.[246]

Due to this event, Forrest would be kept from attacking Sherman's supply line again. If and when Forrest was to defeat a Union army, Sherman had another army ready to move so that they might try their hand with Forrest. Sherman keeping Forrest busy regardless of whether Forrest won still proved successful for Sherman when it came to his supply line. By the beginning of September 1864, Atlanta had fallen to Sherman and his armies.

The war would finally come to a close in 1865. Soldiers would go back into their communities and try to pick up where they had left off before the war came. As the soldiers grew older, some would write their memoirs, become involved with veterans' groups and visit the places where battles raged in order to remember lost friends and past events. Henry George of Lyon's Kentucky brigade did just that. On one occasion, Henry procured a horse and rode down the same road he recalled when Lyon's men moved on Brice's Crossroads. The first placement of the artillery was easily noticeable, yet the cotton gin just down the way was gone. Brice's Crossroads had changed very little, including the right of the road, where the large trees "that were standing then are all scarred with bullets." Henry stayed overnight at the Brice home, recalling, "While it has been kept in good repair, it has the same weather-boarding punctured with holes made by the minnie balls." The old church was gone, with a new one built just across the road. He recalled various buildings still standing, including the log cabin on the ridge near the Tishomingo Creek and bridge. After visiting many of the past battlefields, Henry spoke of Brice's Crossroads battlefield, saying, "No other has been so little defaced as this one." Henry, in looking around and letting the memories

The monument to the Battle of Brice's Crossroads on the northeast corner of Brice's Crossroads. *Author's collection.*

flood back like the Confederate tide that covered Brice's Crossroads on that sweltering day in June, realized, "It has been truthfully said that battle fields may seem on the historical page to be fields of glory, but in reality they are most horrid scenes. While I am writing this my mind runs back to that awful day, and the terrible scenes are almost as vividly in my mind as if they had occurred but yesterday."[247]

Henry understood what Brice's Crossroads meant to him and those who fought there. He also understood the pain and reality of war regardless of victory or defeat. As at Brice's Crossroads, everything came at a price. Today, the battlefield is quiet and peaceful. Few tablets and monuments dot the land. The Tishomingo Creek continues to meander through the battlefield, and the areas that were once Union and Confederate battle lines are now just undulating landscapes. It is difficult to believe such an incredible encounter happened on this peaceful landscape so many years ago in northeast Mississippi. To visit Brice's Crossroads is not to glorify war but to honor the men—Union and Confederate—for their courage, determination and sacrifice and for us to contemplate the costs of war.

Appendix A

Union Order of Battle

Department of the Tennessee, Major General James B. McPherson
District of West Tennessee, Major General Cadwallader C. Washburn
Sturgis's Expeditionary Force, Brigadier General Samuel D. Sturgis

INFANTRY DIVISION, COLONEL WILLIAM L. MCMILLEN

First Brigade, Colonel Alexander Wilkin

114TH ILLINOIS INFANTRY, Lieutenant Colonel J.F. King
93RD INDIANA INFANTRY, Colonel D.C. Thomas
9TH MINNESOTA INFANTRY, Lieutenant Colonel J.F. Marsh
72ND OHIO INFANTRY, Lieutenant Colonel C.G. Eaton
95TH OHIO INFANTRY, Lieutenant Colonel J. Brumback
COMPANY E, 1ST ILLINOIS LIGHT ARTILLERY (four guns), Captain J.A. Fitch
6TH INDIANA BATTERY (section) (two guns), Captain M. Mueller

Second Brigade, Colonel George B. Hoge

81ST ILLINOIS INFANTRY, Colonel F. Campbell, Lieutenant Colonel A.W. Rogers
95TH ILLINOIS INFANTRY, Colonel T.W. Humphrey, Captain W.H. Stewart, Captain E.W. Bush, Captain A. Shellenberger

108TH ILLINOIS INFANTRY, Lieutenant Colonel R.L. Sidwell

113TH ILLINOIS INFANTRY, Lieutenant Colonel G.R. Clarke

120TH ILLINOIS INFANTRY, Colonel G.W. McKeaig, Lieutenant Colonel S.B. Floyd

COMPANY B, 2ND ILLINOIS LIGHT ARTILLERY (four guns), Captain F.H. Chapman

Third Brigade, Colonel Edward Bouton

55TH U.S. COLORED INFANTRY, Major E.M. Lowe; Captain A.T. Reeves

59TH U.S. COLORED INFANTRY, Lieutenant Colonel R. Cowden, Captain J.C. Foster

COMPANY F, 2ND U.S. COLORED ARTILLERY (two guns), Captain C.A. Lamberg

CAVALRY DIVISION, BRIGADIER GENERAL BENJAMIN H. GRIERSON

First Brigade, Colonel George E. Waring

7TH INDIANA CAVALRY, Lieutenant Colonel T.M. Browne

3RD AND 9TH ILLINOIS CAVALRY (detachment), Captain A.A. Mock

4TH MISSOURI CAVALRY (four mountain howitzers), Lieutenant Colonel G. von Heimrich

2ND NEW JERSEY CAVALRY, Colonel J. Kargé

19TH PENNSYLVANIA CAVALRY, Lieutenant Colonel J.C. Hess

Second Brigade, Colonel Edward F. Winslow

7TH ILLINOIS CAVALRY (detachment)

3RD IOWA CAVALRY, Lieutenant Colonel John W. Noble

4TH IOWA CAVALRY, Major Abial R. Pierce

10TH MISSOURI CAVALRY (detachment) (two guns), Major M.H. Williams

7TH WISCONSIN BATTERY (section) (two guns), Captain H.S. Lee

Information taken from Bearss, *Forrest at Brice's Crossroads*, 347–48

Confederate Order of Battle

Department of Alabama, Mississippi and East Louisiana, Major General Stephen D. Lee
Forrest's Cavalry Corps, Major General Nathan B. Forrest
Buford's Division, Brigadier General Abraham Buford

THIRD BRIGADE, COLONEL HYLAN B. LYON

3RD KENTUCKY MOUNTED INFANTRY, Lieutenant Colonel G.A.C. Holt
7TH KENTUCKY MOUNTED INFANTRY, Lieutenant Colonel L.J. Sherrill
8TH KENTUCKY MOUNTED INFANTRY, Lieutenant Colonel A.R. Shackett
12TH KENTUCKY CAVALRY, Major T.S. Tate

FOURTH BRIGADE, COLONEL TYREE H. BELL

2ND TENNESSEE CAVALRY, Colonel C.R. Barteau
16TH TENNESSEE CAVALRY, Colonel A.N. Wilson
19TH TENNESSEE CAVALRY, Colonel J.F. Newsom
20TH TENNESSEE CAVALRY, Colonel R.M. Russell

Appendix B

Sixth Brigade, Colonel Edmund Rucker

8th Mississippi Cavalry, Colonel W.L. Duff
18th Mississippi Cavalry Battalion, Lieutenant Colonel A.H. Chalmers
7th Tennessee Cavalry, Colonel W.L. Duckworth

Johnson's Brigade, Colonel William A. Johnson

4th Alabama Cavalry, Lieutenant Colonel F.M. Windes
Moreland's Alabama cavalry regiment, Major J.N. George
William's Alabama cavalry battalion, Captain J.F. Doan
Warren's Alabama cavalry battalion, Captain W.H. Warren

Artillery, Captain John W. Morton

Morton's Tennessee Battery (four guns), Lieutenant T. Saunders Sale
Rice's Tennessee Battery (four guns), Captain T.W. Rice

Information taken from Bearss, *Forrest at Brice's Crossroads*, 348–49

Notes

CHAPTER 1

1. Cogley, *History of the Seventh Indiana Cavalry*, 107.
2. Grant, *Personal Memoirs*, 2: 114–25.
3. Sherman, *Memoirs*, 2: 24–26.
4. Grant, *Personal Memoirs*, 2: 120.
5. Sherman, *Memoirs*, 2: 15–21, 24.
6. Ibid., 2: 9.
7. Ibid.
8. U.S. War Department, *War of the Rebellion*, ser. 1, vol. 39, 2: 116. Hereafter cited as *OR*.
9. Johnston. Narrative of Military Operations, 262–63.
10. Ibid., 318.
11. Lee, *Battle of Brice's Crossroads*, 27–28. It should be noted that an official report of this engagement by General Stephen D. Lee was not completed or has not been found at this time. Lee's publication for the Mississippi Historical Society appears to be his report; however, it is written in 1902, which is years after the war and death of General Forrest.
12. Lee, *Battle of Brice's Crossroads*, 6: 28.
13. *OR*, ser. 1, vol. 39, 2: 3–4, 10, 12.
14. Sherman, *Memoirs*, 2: 31, 52.
15. *OR*, vol. 38, 4: 9, 3.
16. Ibid., vol. 32, 3: 415, 411.

17. Waugh, *Class of 1846*, xiv–xv.
18. One story of how Sturgis may have become a prisoner at that time came from Samuel Chamberlain. Sturgis was possibly a lieutenant at the time of being made prisoner. Chamberlain was there at the time and recalled, "Lieut. Sturgis, ordering Serg't Mellen to occupy the rancho and not to leave it, with his orderly started in pursuit. We could see them ride up as far as they could, and then dismount and lead their horses up until they were hid behind the summit, when we heard the reports of several shots…All the 'hombras' in the place were made prisoners and confined in a house under guard." Chamberlain, *My Confession*, 147.
19. One account mentions Sturgis chasing Chief Joseph and the Nez Perces in a running gun battle in which Sturgis "drove on through the bare and broken country. Overcharged and obsessed, he outdid himself. He covered thirty-seven miles, but his command was spread out over the landscape for ten miles and one-third of it was on foot." Hagemann, *Fighting Rebels*, 36.
20. Maury, *Recollections of a Virginian*, 113.
21. Waugh, *Class of 1846*, 146–49.
22. Brooksher, *Bloody Hill*, 222–23, 225.
23. Dillon, letter to Dr. G.A. Gessner, Gessner Collection, 151.
24. Haupt, *Reminiscences*, 80, 83; Warner, *Generals in Blue*, 487.
25. Gould, *Story of the Forty-eighth*, 97, 99; O'Reilly, *Fredericksburg Campaign*, 350.
26. Warner, *Generals in Blue*, 487.
27. *OR*, vol. 32, 3: 527.
28. Ibid., vol. 32, 3:484; Bearss, *Forrest at Brice's Crossroads*, 6–8.
29. Bearss, *Forrest at Brice's Crossroads*, 8; *OR*, vol. 32, 1: 698.
30. *OR*, vol. 32, 3: 536.
31. Warner, *Generals in Gray*, 92–93; Wills, *Battle from the Start*, 113–16.
32. Wyeth, *Life of General Nathan Bedford Forrest*, 264–66.
33. Warner, *Generals in Gray*, 92.
34. *OR*, vol. 32, 1: 695–96.
35. Ibid.
36. Ibid., vol. 32, 3: 819, 822, 854.
37. Ibid., vol. 32, 1: 697.
38. McCarty and McCarty, *Chatfield Story*, 342.
39. *OR*, vol. 32, 1: 698–701.
40. Ibid., vol. 32, 1: 694–95.
41. Ibid., vol. 39, 2: 29–30.
42. Ibid., vol. 39, 2: 601, 614, 618; Wills, *Battle from the Start*, 201–2.

Chapter 2

43. *OR*, vol. 39, 2: 33, 41–43, 49.
44. Ibid., vol. 39, 2: 49, 55.
45. Bearss, *Forrest at Brice's Crossroads*, 40–41; *OR*, vol. 39, 2: 58–59.
46. *OR*, vol. 39, 2: 41, 53, 58.
47. Ibid., vol. 39, 1: 217–18.
48. Ibid., vol. 39, 1: 218.
49. Bearss, *Forrest at Brice's Crossroads*, 41; *OR*, vol. 39, 1: 215–17.
50. Bearss, *Forrest at Brice's Crossroads*, 41; *OR*, vol. 39, 1: 215–16.
51. Dinges and Leckie, *Just and Righteous Cause*, 235.
52. Morton, *Artillery of Nathan Bedford Forrest's Cavalry*, 172.
53. Lee, *Battle of Brice's Crossroads*, 6: 29–30.
54. *OR*, vol. 39, 1: 221–22.
55. Ibid., vol. 39, 1: 222.
56. Lee, *Battle of Brice's Crossroads*, 6: 30.
57. Ibid.; Hughes, *Brigadier General Tyree H. Bell*, 137; *OR*, vol. 39, 1: 222.
58. *OR*, vol. 39, 1: 148–49, 152; Dinges and Leckie, *Just and Righteous Cause*, 237.
59. Cogley, *History of the Seventh Indiana Cavalry*, 99.
60. *OR*, vol. 39, 1: 149, 172.
61. Ibid., vol. 39, 1: 149.
62. Dinges and Leckie, *Just and Righteous Cause*, 237; *OR*, vol. 39, 1: 90.
63. Cogley, *History of the Seventh Indiana Cavalry*, 99–100.
64. Ibid., 100.
65. McCarty and McCarty, *Chatfield Story*, 352; Bartleson, partial diary, 21.
66. *OR*, vol. 39, 1: 91.
67. Dinges and Leckie, *Just and Righteous Cause*, 240. McMillen would later state, "I would rather go on and meet the enemy, even if we should be whipped, than to return to Memphis without having met them." *OR*, vol. 39, 1: 207.
68. *OR*, vol. 39, 1: 91.
69. Hancock, *Hancock's Diary*, 378–80.
70. *OR*, vol. 39, 1: 222, Morton, *Artillery of Nathan Bedford Forrest's Cavalry*, 173–74.
71. Morgan, *Artillery of Nathan Bedford Forrest's Cavalry*, 174; Lee, *Battle of Brice's Crossroads*, 32.
72. Lee, *Battle of Brice's Crossroads*, 31–32. Bell also remembered the conversation between Lee and Forrest, stating, "The understanding was

very specific that Gen. Forrest should not bring on an engagement but retire in front of the federal forces, skirmish with them until they could be drawn into the prairie country above Okolona." Bell, *Autobiography*, 51–52.

73. Wyeth, *Life of Lieutenant-General Nathan Bedford Forrest*, 399.

74. Ibid., 398–400.

75. Lee, *Battle of Brice's Crossroads*, 30–33; *OR*, vol. 39, 1: 222; Morgan, *Artillery of Nathan Bedford Forrest's Cavalry*, 174.

76. *OR*, vol. 39, 1: 153.

77. Dinges and Leckie, *Just and Righteous Cause*, 240–41.

Chapter 3

78. Skaptason, "West Tennessee U.S. Colored Troops," 79; *OR*, vol. 39, 1:172; Dinges and Leckie, *Just and Righteous Cause*, 242–43.

79. Dinges and Leckie, *Just and Righteous Cause*, 243; *OR*, vol. 39, 1: 92. Major E.M. Lowe also recalled the meeting between Sturgis and Grierson, in which he believed the very words of Sturgis to be, "General, you will advance with all of your command, consisting of all the cavalry, and fell the enemy carefully, and remember that Forrest is a cunning and wily foe, and as you advance select a battle ground, and advise me by sending back an aide to lead the infantry into position." According to Lowe, "Gen. Grierson engaged Forrest and got himself a whipping." These statements would bring upon Lowe the ire of many from the cavalry units in the years to come. Gessner Collection, Box 3, Compilation of accounts entitled, "General Sturgis at Guntown, Miss., (1864), Letter to the *Toledo Blade*, 1.

80. *OR*, vol. 39, 1: 92, 168.

81. Hancock, *Hancock's Diary*, 382.

82. Morton, *Artillery of Nathan Bedford Forrest's Cavalry*, 174; Mathes. *General Forrest*, 238–39, 241; Jordan and Pryor, *Campaigns of Lieut-Gen. N.B. Forrest*, 467–69; *OR*, vol. 39, 1: 222–23, 225.

83. George, *History of the 3d, 7th, 8th and 12th Kentucky C.S.A.*, 92.

84. *OR*, vol. 39, 1: 129, 132, 222.

85. Ibid., vol. 39, 1: 222–23, Mathes, *General Forrest*, 241.

86. Bell, *Autobiography*, 52.

87. Hancock, *Hancock's Diary*, 382–83.

88. George, *History of the 3rd, 7th, 8th and 12th Kentucky C.S.A.*, 88–89.

89. Brown, "Guntown or Brice's X Roads Fight," 556; *OR*, vol. 39, 1: 223; George. *History of the 3d, 7th, 8th and 12th Kentucky C.S.A.*, 91; Bearss, *Forrest at Brice's Crossroads*, 69; Hord, "Brice's X Roads," 529. Colonel Hylan B. Lyon's 3rd, 7th and 8th Kentuckians were referred to as mounted infantry, while the 12th Kentucky was referred to as cavalry.

90. Hancock, *Hancock's Diary*, 383; George. *History of the 3rd, 7th, 8th and 12th Kentucky C.S.A.*, 90.

91. Agnew, "Battle of Tishomingo Creek," 2.

92. George, *History of the 3rd, 7th, 8th and 12th Kentucky C.S.A.*, 90.

93. Jordan and Pryor, *Campaigns of Lieut-Gen. N.B. Forrest*, 468; *OR*, vol. 39, 1: 223.

94. Brown, "Guntown or Brice's X Roads Fight," 556.

95. Morton, *Artillery of Nathan Bedford Forrest's Cavalry*, 175; Bell. *Autobiography*, 52.

96. Mathes, *General Forrest*, 240; Brice, "Brice's Cross Roads," 1; Wyeth, *Life of Lieutenant-General Nathan Bedford Forrest*, 403; Scott, *Story of a Cavalry Regiment*, 236–37.

97. Mathes, *General Forrest*, 240; Wyeth, *Life of Lieutenant-General Nathan Bedford Forrest*, 403; Scott, *Story of a Cavalry Regiment*, 236–37.

98. Dinges and Leckie, *Just and Righteous Cause*, 244; *OR*, vol. 39, 1: 129, 132.

99. *OR*, vol. 39, 1: 129, 132, 139. It should be noted that the 3rd Illinois Cavalry consisted of a detachment of 20 men, while the 9th Illinois Cavalry was a detachment of 140 men and had just returned from a veteran furlough. Captain A.R. Mock was in overall command of both detachments. Bailey, "Guntown," 3.

100. George, *History of the 3rd, 7th, 8th and 12th Kentucky C.S.A.*, 90; Jordan and Pryor, *Campaigns of Lieut-Gen. N.B. Forrest*, 468.

101. Bearss, *Forrest at Brice's Crossroads*, 72; Jordan and Pryor, *Campaigns of Lieut-Gen. N.B. Forrest*, 470; *OR*, vol. 39, 1: 223.

102. *OR*, vol. 39, 1: 223.

103. Cogley, *History of the Seventh Indiana Cavalry*, 102; *OR*, vol. 39, 1: 135.

104. *OR*, vol. 39, 1: 72, 135.

105. Cogley, *History of the Seventh Indiana Cavalry*, 112; *OR*, vol. 39, 1: 135.

106. *OR*, vol. 39, 1: 135; Wyeth, *Life of Lieutenant-General Nathan Bedford Forrest*, 406; Johnson, Buel and Hanson, "Forrest's Defeat of Sturgis," 420.

107. *OR*, vol. 39, 1: 135; Bearss, *Forrest at Brice's Crossroads*, 75. In Colonel Waring's official report, he wrote concerning the reserves at the time of the battle that "the Second New Jersey Cavalry, under Lieutenant-Colonel Kitchen, was in reserve in position to re-enforce the right wing

should it be endangered." He then explained, "The first of these assaults was repulsed; the second one, after a hand-to-hand fight, was successful, and forced back my right, although the whole Second New Jersey and reserve of the Seventh Indiana were brought into action." These reserves were brought into action on the far left instead of reinforcing the Seventh Indiana Cavalry, where they were sorely needed. However, in defense of Waring, the dense natural foliage helped to mask the Confederate troop numbers to the extent that Waring and the others had a difficult time making reserve decisions. *OR*, vol. 39, 1: 132.

108. Cogley, *History of the Seventh Indiana Cavalry*, 112–13; *OR*, vol. 39, 1: 135.

109. Cogley, *History of the Seventh Indiana Cavalry*, 113.

110. Dinges and Leckie, *Just and Righteous Cause*, 245; Johnson, Buel and Hanson, "Forrest's Defeat of Sturgis," 420.

111. *OR*, vol. 39, 1: 223; Bearss, *Forrest at Brice's Crossroads*, 71; Johnson, Buel and Hanson, "Forrest's Defeat of Sturgis," 420; Dinges and Leckie, *Just and Righteous Cause*, 245. Grierson's estimate of Confederate troops being placed from six to seven thousand was quite possibly due to false estimates given by area citizens. In one case, Grierson stated that the numbers from the citizens were the following: "Forrest's whole command, consisting of 7,000 or 8,000 men and six pieces of artillery, had passed." *OR*, vol. 39, 1: 200.

112. Dinges and Leckie, *Just and Righteous Cause*, 244; *OR*, vol. 39, 1: 204.

113. *OR*, vol. 39, 1: 137, 129; Dinges and Leckie, *Just and Righteous Cause*, 244; letter to Gessner, February 8 1881, Gessner Collection, Private James H. White, Company H, 3rd Iowa Cavalry, vol. 4, 625.

114. *OR*, vol. 39, 1: 184–85.

CHAPTER 4

115. *OR*, vol. 39, 1: 184–85, 187.

116. Ibid., vol. 39, 1: 137, 141; Young, *Seventh Tennessee Cavalry*, 90. Charles W. Sherman, who was a sergeant in Company K, 3rd Iowa Cavalry, wrote years later of a possible opportunity lost, stating, "I sent word by my captain that the edge of the woods beyond the brush a half mile beyond where the first line was actually formed was the best place to form our line, and a charge of cavalry if made then or soon after, before the rebs were fully formed would win us a victory. But instead a few moments later we were ordered back and the regiment was dismounted and formed in line on the right of the road, on top of the rising ground." Sergeant

Sherman would be captured after the battle near Ripley, Mississippi, but go on to serve out the remainder of the war. Gessner Collection, letter of Sergeant Charles W. Sherman, Company K, 3rd Iowa Cavalry, vol. 4, 603.

117. Witherspoon, *Tishomingo Creek*, 3–4.

118. Ibid., 5.

119. Young, *Seventh Tennessee Cavalry*, 90–91; Hubbard, *Notes of a Private*, 98; Henry, *As They Saw Forrest*, 163.

120. Henry, *As They Saw Forrest*, 163.

121. Gessner Collection, letter of Private Joseph McCaulley, February 20, 1882, Company E, 3rd Iowa Cavalry, vol. 4, 549.

122. Gessner Collection, letter of Captain Eldred Huff, February 20, 1882, Company A, 4th Iowa Cavalry, vol. 4, 727.

123. Hord, "Brice's X Roads," 529.

124. Jordan and Pryor, *Campaigns of Lieut-Gen. N.B. Forrest*, 470–71; Hills, "Study in Warfighting," 28.

125. Bearss, *Forrest at Brice's Crossroads*, 75–76; *OR*, vol. 39, 1: 141–42, 144, 204; Scott, *Story of a Cavalry Regiment*, 243.

126. *OR*, vol. 39, 1:92, 141, 2: 97. Interestingly, this was the only message of correspondence within the *Official Records* between Sturgis and Grierson during this time of the fighting. Their after-action reports and testimonies before the court of inquiry, along with Grierson's memoir, are the primary sources for their exchanges concerning what was in the messages sent between the two before and during the battle.

127. *OR*, vol. 39, 1: 92, 129, 153, 200.

128. Ibid., vol. 39, 1: 92, 153.

129. Ibid., vol. 39, 1: 92, 153, 200.

130. Ibid., vol. 39, 1: 92.

131. *OR*, vol. 39, 1: 201; Dinges and Leckie, *Just and Righteous Cause*, 245.

132. Dinges and Leckie, *Just and Righteous Cause*, 246.

133. *OR*, vol. 39, 1: 223.

134. Dinges and Leckie, *Just and Righteous Cause*, 246.

135. Ibid.; *OR*, vol. 39, 1: 153–54.

136. *OR*, vol. 39, 1: 92–93; Dinges and Leckie, *Just and Righteous Cause*, 246. Grierson believed that it was around 2:00 p.m. when the infantry started to arrive at the crossroads and another half hour before they moved into the line of battle that had been occupied by the cavalry.

137. *OR*, vol. 39, 1: 103–4.

138. Ibid., vol. 39, 1: 104, 118.

139. Ibid., vol. 39, 1: 118–19.

140. Gessner Collection, letter from J.H. Mooney, February 20, 1882, Company E, 113th Illinois Infantry Regiment.

141. *OR*, vol. 39, 1: 124; Wood. *History of the Ninety-Fifth Regiment Illinois Infantry*, 110; *OR*, vol. 39, 1: 116–17; Gessner Collection, Box 3, Compilation of accounts entitled "General Sturgis at Guntown, Miss. (1864)," letter to the editor, *Cleveland Leader*, 17.

142. *OR*, vol. 39, 1: 121; Gessner Collection, Box 3, Compilation of accounts entitled "General Sturgis at Guntown, Miss. (1864)," letter to Chaplain William S. Post, 46–47.

143. *OR*, vol. 39, 1: 107, 103.

144. Lacock, "Guntown Trip," 1; *OR*, vol. 39, 1: 107.

145. Cowden, *Brief Sketch of the Fifty-Ninth Regiment of United States Colored Infantry*, 93; *OR*, vol. 39, 1: 125.

Chapter 5

146. *OR*, vol. 39, 1: 223; Morgan, *Artillery of Nathan Bedford Forrest's Cavalry*, 176.

147. George, *History of the 3rd, 7th, 8th and 12th Kentucky C.S.A.*, 93.

148. Bell, *Autobiography*, 52. Forrest would write in his report that he "wrote back to General Buford to move up with the artillery and Bell's brigade as rapidly as the condition of the horses and roads would permit, and ordered him also to send one regiment of Bell's brigade from Old Carrollville across to the Ripley and Guntown road, with orders to gain the rear of the enemy or attack and annoy his rear or flank." This would mean that Forrest ordered the regiment in Bell's brigade to gain the rear of the Union army much sooner than Bell wrote. Hancock also wrote, "A courier was also dispatched with instructions to Buford to detach a regiment at Carrollville to gain the Federal rear, and, if possible, destroy their train." Regardless, the attack was made with the expected results. *OR*, vol. 39, 1: 223; Hancock, *Hancock's Diary*, 382–83, 390–91.

149. *OR*, vol. 39, 1: 223; George, *History of the 3rd, 7th, 8th and 12th Kentucky C.S.A.*, 92–93; Bell, *Autobiography*, 61.

150. Henry, *As They Saw Forrest*, 163–64.

151. *OR*, vol. 39, 1: 208; Bearss, *Forrest at Brice's Crossroads*, 81.

152. *OR*, vol. 39, 1: 104; Gessner Collection, Box 3, compilation of accounts entitled "General Sturgis at Guntown, Miss. (1864)," interview with Colonel George B. Hoge, March 1, 61–62.

153. *OR*, vol. 39, 1: 119.

154. Ibid., vol. 39, 1: 107, 104.

155. Ibid., vol. 39, 1: 104.

156. Ibid.

157. Ibid., vol. 39, 1: 144l Gessner Collection, Box 3, compilation of accounts entitled "General Sturgis at Guntown, Miss. (1864)," letter to the editor of the *Toledo Blade* from H. Ramsey, March 24, 1879, 4; Gessner Collection, Box 3, compilation of accounts entitled "General Sturgis at Guntown, Miss. (1864)," letter to G.A. Gessner from John W. Jenkins, January 24, 1882, 32; Gessner Collection, Box 3, compilation of accounts entitled "General Sturgis at Guntown, Miss. (1864)," letter to G.A. Gessner from William Roarke, January 15, 1882, 43; Gessner Collection, letter of R.S. Patten to G.A. Gessner, March 7, 1882, Company B, 114th Illinois Infantry; Waring, *Whip and Spur*, 130.

158. Wyeth, *Life of Lieutenant-General Nathan Bedford Forrest*, 412; Jordan and Pryor, *Campaigns of Lieut-Gen. N.B. Forrest*, 472.

159. Wyeth, *Life of Lieutenant-General Nathan Bedford Forrest*, 413.

160. *OR*, vol. 39, 1: 223; Jordan and Pryor, *Campaigns of Lieut-Gen. N.B. Forrest*, 472.

161. Bell, *Autobiography*, 61; Hughes, *Brigadier General Tyree H. Bell*, 142.

162. Bell, *Autobiography*, 61–62. Tyree Bell's son Isaac would receive severe wounds to his left arm and side but live to fight another day. Hughes, *Brigadier General Tyree H. Bell*, 143.

163. Grierson would state that he did not withdraw Winslow's troops based on the fact that he believed a "fierce attack had been made on the right of our line and the infantry was a long time in getting into position." He went on to advise Sturgis, "In my judgment, it would not be judicious to withdraw Winslow's brigade until a larger force of infantry could be brought up and placed in line of battle." To add to the stress and confusion, Sturgis received a report that the cavalry horses were becoming an obstruction. This caused Sturgis to immediately send out an order directed to Winslow to "withdraw, or fall back, and get his horses out of the way of the infantry." Dinges and Leckie, *Just and Righteous Cause*, 246–47.

164. Scott, *Story of a Cavalry Regiment*, 245; *OR*, vol. 39, 1: 129, 137, 204; Bearss, *Forrest at Brice's Crossroads*, 88–89. It is difficult to understand why Sturgis allowed the larger cavalry regiments of the 3rd and 4th Iowa to move off the battlefield during such a crucial time in the battle. Perhaps it was the stress, coupled with the constant reminders from Grierson that his

men were worn out and low on ammunition. If this were true, it should be questioned why Grierson would allow the 10th Missouri and 7th Illinois Cavalry, which were considered the weaker cavalry regiments due to size, such an important task as holding the Union right. It would seem more logical to move the two Iowa cavalry regiments into this position. Fog of war and the heat of battle play their part in the stress and decisions of war. Grierson would later admit, "It was a great mistake to withdraw the cavalry. It should have been continued in action and more infantry brought to its support, and particularly Winslow's brigade, which had so long successfully fought the enemy." Furthermore he believed, "Had it been retained, and Bouton's brigade and the balance of Wilkin's [brigade] brought forward and put into action, we could have gained the victory, or at least held our ground and position at the crossroads until night, and either strengthened our lines then or gotten into shape for a battle the next day." Dinges and Leckie, *Just and Righteous Cause*, 247.

165. Dinges and Leckie, *Just and Righteous Cause*, 246–47.

166. Ibid., 247–48; *OR*, vol. 39, 1:129; Scott, *Story of a Cavalry Regiment*, 245.

167. *OR*, vol. 39, 1: 111, 169, 223.

168. Ibid., vol. 39, 1: 111, 169, 209, 223; George, *History of the 3rd, 7th, 8th and 12th Kentucky C.S.A.*, 93.

169. *OR*, vol. 39, 1: 111, 169, 209; Bearss, *Forrest at Brice's Crossroads*, 90; George, *History of the 3rd, 7th, 8th and 12th Kentucky C.S.A.*, 93–94.

170. Minnesota Board of Commissioners, *Minnesota in the Civil and Indian Wars*, 2: 465.

171. Ibid.; Bearss, *Forrest at Brice's Crossroads*, 90.

172. Minnesota Board of Commissioners, *Minnesota in the Civil and Indian Wars*, 2: 465–66; MacDonald, "Battle of Brice's Cross Roads," 6: 453.

173. Wilkin, letter, "Dear Sarah," vol. 39, 1: 112.

CHAPTER 6

174. Scott, *Story of a Cavalry Regiment*, 245; Dinges and Leckie, *Just and Righteous Cause*, 247–48.

175. *OR*, vol. 39, 1: 154.

176. Ibid., vol. 39, 1: 154–55. Interestingly, Major Edgar M. Lowe would, years later, come to Sturgis's defense in the case of the wagon train arriving on the battlefield. He would come to admit, "But there are some things that I know Gen. Sturgis is not guilty of; one is, of rushing the

wagons to the front and in the way of the troops for be it remembered, I was in command of the train guard and I aver that when I got the order to hurry to the front, I distinctly ordered the Chief Wagonmaster to park his train where I had left him, and to remain there until ordered to move; and I was never more surprised in my life when I found the train within less than a half mile of the line of battle. I think now and, have thought for many years that I ought to have left a guard to enforce that order." Lowe, "At Guntown," 3.

177. Gessner Collection, letter of Sergeant John Jones to G.A. Gessner, March 27, 1882, Company E, 4th Iowa Cavalry; Scott, *Story of a Cavalry Regiment*, 246–47.

178. *OR*, vol. 39, 1: 173.

179. Ibid.; Bearss, *Forrest at Brice's Crossroads*, 89–90.

180. *OR*, vol. 39, 1: 173.

181. Wyeth, *Life of Lieutenant-General Nathan Bedford Forrest*, 414; Bell, *Autobiography*, 62; *OR*, vol. 39, 1: 223.

182. Wyeth, *Life of Lieutenant-General Nathan Bedford Forrest*, 414; *OR*, vol. 39, 1: 119–20, 163–64; Hubbard, *Notes of a Private*, 99–100; Gessner Collection, Box 3, compilation of accounts entitled "General Sturgis at Guntown, Miss. (1864)," interview with Colonel George B. Hoge, March 1, 62; *OR*, vol. 20, 1: 972–73. The Sons of Confederate Veterans created a medal recently to recognize those who had earned the Roll of Honor distinction. One was awarded posthumously for Columbus K. Hall. The medal is on permanent display at the Brice's Crossroads Visitor Center. Hall, "Sergeant Columbus K. Hall," 16–18.

183. *OR*, vol. 39, 1: 223.

184. Ibid., vol. 39, 1: 163–64.

185. Ibid., vol. 39, 1: 121; Bearss, *Forrest at Brice's Crossroads*, 90; Bartleson, partial diary, 22–23.

186. *OR*, vol. 39, 1: 121–22; Bartleson, partial diary, 23–24; Orr, "Guntown Again," 1.

187. Captain Edmund Newsome of Company B knew what had happened to the adjutant, recalling, "We ran out of ammunition. The adjutant went back for ammunition and had to go far back to find an ammunition wagon. He forced one to come up near and supplied us again after we began to fall back." Edmund Newsom, letter to Dr. G.A. Gessner.

188. *OR*, vol. 39, 1: 121–22.

189. Brice, "Brice's Cross Roads," 3.

190. Wood, *History of the Ninety-Fifth Regiment Illinois Infantry*, 111–12.

191. Gessner Collection, Box 3, compilation of accounts entitled "General Sturgis at Guntown, Miss. (1864)," letter to the *Chicago Tribune*, 50.

192. *OR*, vol. 39, 1: 124; Gessner Collection, letter from J.H. Mooney to G.A. Gessner.

193. *OR*, vol. 39, 1: 163; Beach, *Recollections and Extracts*, 29–30; Gessner Collection, letter from J.H. Mooney to G.A. Gessner.

194. *OR*, vol. 39, 1: 116–17, 119–20.

195. Ibid., vol. 39, 1: 124; Beach, *Recollections and Extracts*, 30.

196. Hancock, *Hancock's Diary*, 390–92.

197. *OR*, vol. 39, 1: 114–15; Bearss, *Forrest at Brice's Crossroads*, 93; Wyeth, *Life of Lieutenant-General Nathan Bedford Forrest*, 415.

198. Wyeth, *Life of Lieutenant-General Nathan Bedford Forrest*, 414–15.

199. Ibid., 415.

200. Ibid., 415–16, Bearss, *Forrest at Brice's Crossroads*, 71, 94; Henry, *First with the Most*, 288.

201. *OR*, vol. 39, 1: 93.

202. Wyeth. *Life of Lieutenant-General Nathan Bedford Forrest*, 415–16.

203. *OR*, vol. 39, 1: 93, 155; Beach, *Recollections and Extracts*, 30.

204. *OR*, vol. 39, 1: 105; Bearss, *Forrest at Brice's Crossroads*, 95.

205. *OR*, vol. 39, 1: 105; Hord, "Brice's X Roads," 529–30.

206. Brown, "Guntown or Brice's X Roads Fight," 556; George, "Brice's Cross Roads," 3.

207. Bartleson, partial diary, 25–26.

208. Wyeth, *Life of Lieutenant-General Nathan Bedford Forrest*, 416; Bearss, *Forrest at Brice's Crossroads*, 71, 97.

209. *OR*, vol. 39, 1: 112, 117, 169.

210. Ibid., vol. 39, 1: 195.

211. Ibid., vol. 39, 1: 186; Morgan, *Artillery of Nathan Bedford Forrest's Cavalry*, 176; Bearss, *Forrest at Brice's Crossroads*, 100.

212. Hubbard, *Notes of a Private*, 100–1; Jordan and Pryor, *Campaigns of Lieut-Gen. N.B. Forrest*, 477.

213. *OR*, vol. 39, 1: 105, 107, 213; Lowe. "At Guntown," 3; Cowde, *Brief Sketch of the Fifty-Ninth Regiment of United States Colored Infantry*, 78; Bearss, *Forrest at Brice's Crossroads*, 101.

214. Cowden, *Brief Sketch of the Fifty-Ninth Regiment of United States Colored Infantry*, 79; Hord. "Brice's X Roads," 530; *OR*, vol. 39, 1: 224; Jordan and Pryor, *Campaigns of Lieut-Gen. N.B. Forrest*, 475.

215. *OR*, vol. 39, 1: 115, 145, 175, 210,; Wyeth, *Life of Lieutenant-General Nathan Bedford Forrest*, 418; Scott, *Story of a Cavalry Regiment*, 247–49; Bearss, *Forrest*

at Brice's Crossroads, 102. Major Edgar M. Lowe also commented on the last organized troops from the Guntown battlefield: "I most emphatically say that all the white troops were in full retreat at the time, while the colored troops were yet in line of battle, and that the colored troops remained there for nearly an hour after all the white troops were gone, and only retreated when the rebels were in front and on both flanks." Lowe, "At Guntown," 3.

Chapter 7

216. *OR*, vol. 39, 1: 115; Dinges and Leckie, *Just and Righteous Cause*, 250.

217. Bearss, *Forrest at Brice's Crossroads*, 108–10; *OR*, vol. 39, 1: 126, 181–82; Cowden, *Brief Sketch of the Fifty-Ninth Regiment of United States Colored Infantry*, 93–98.

218. Bearss, *Forrest at Brice's Crossroads*, 108–10; *OR*, vol. 39, 1: 126, 181–82, 198; Cowden, *Brief Sketch of the Fifty-Ninth Regiment of United States Colored Infantry*, 93–98.

219. *OR*, vol. 39, 1: 127, 182, 198; Cowden, *Brief Sketch of the Fifty-Ninth Regiment of United States Colored Infantry*, 97–98.

220. *OR*, vol. 39, 1: 224; Wyeth, *Life of Lieutenant-General Nathan Bedford Forrest*, 419; Henry, *As They Saw Forrest*, 126–27.

221. *OR*, vol. 39, 1: 94, 129; Dinges and Leckie, *Just and Righteous Cause*, 250.

222. Agnew, "Battle of Tishomingo Creek," 2.

223. Bearss, *Forrest at Brice's Crossroads*, 108, 110–12; *OR*, vol. 39, 1: 108, Cowden, *Brief Sketch*, 97–98.

224. *OR*, vol. 39, 1: 108, 174.

225. Bell, *Autobiography*, 53–54.

226. Ibid., 54; Morton, *Artillery of Nathan Bedford Forrest's Cavalry*, 178–80; Bearss, *Forrest at Brice's Crossroads*, 111–12; Minnesota Board of Commissioners, *Minnesota in the Civil and Indian Wars*, 2: 466; *OR*, vol. 39, 1: 108.

227. Bell, *Autobiography*, 54–55; *OR*, vol. 39, 1: 108, 126; Wilkin, letter, "Dear Sarah."

228. *OR*, vol. 39, 1: 224.

229. Wilkin, letter, "Dear Sarah"; *OR*, vol. 39, 1: 108, 224; Gessner Collection, Box 3, compilation of accounts entitled "General Sturgis at Guntown, Miss. (1864)," letter to Rev. Wm. S. Post, DD, 47–49.

230. *OR*, vol. 39, 1: 186.

231. Wilkin, letter, "Dear Sarah"; *OR*, vol. 39, 1: 108.

232. *OR*, vol. 39, 1: 213–14.

233. Bearss, *Forrest at Brice's Crossroads*, 108; *OR*, vol. 39, 1: 126, 181–82, 198; Cowden, *Brief Sketch of the Fifty-Ninth Regiment of United States Colored Infantry*, 98.

234. *OR*, vol. 39, 1: 226–28.

235. Ibid., vol. 39, 1: 89, 2: 123–24. For the detailed description of the investigation into Sturgis's expedition, see *Proceedings of a Board of Investigation*, *OR*, vol. 39, 1: 147–220, Welsh. *Medical Histories of Union Generals*, 326.

236. Gessner Collection, letter from John M. Magner to G.A. Gessner; Marsh, letter to "My Dear Brother John"; Gessner Collection, Box 3, compilation of accounts entitled "General Sturgis at Guntown, Miss. (1864)," letter to G.A. Gessner from J.C. Allen; Gessner Collection, Box 3, compilation of accounts entitled "General Sturgis at Guntown, Miss. (1864)," letter to wife from soldier, 56–57.

237. Gessner Collection, Box 3, compilation of accounts entitled "General Sturgis at Guntown, Miss. (1864)," letter to G.A. Gessner from D.W.C. Thomas, 60.

238. Dr. Gustavus A. Gessner was a member of the 72nd Ohio Infantry at the time of the Battle of Brice's Crossroads and was taken prisoner. Dr. Gessner became upset with the idea that Sturgis was to be appointed to the position of superintendent of the Soldier's Home in Washington, D.C. He organized a protest among the veterans against Sturgis's appointment. Although the protest failed to stop Sturgis from getting the appointed position, numerous letters from soldiers can be found at the Hayes Presidential Center in Freemont, Ohio. Materials pertaining to the Battle of Guntown can be found in box one, folders one through three, and box three, folder two.

239. Gessner Collection, box 3, compilation of accounts entitled "General Sturgis at Guntown, Miss. (1864)," letter to the *Cleveland Leader*, 39–40, Gessner Collection, Box 3, compilation of accounts entitled "General Sturgis at Guntown, Miss. (1864)," letter to G.A. Gessner from R.B. Thrapp, 51–52.

240. Agnew, "Battle of Tishomingo Creek," 2.

241. Ibid.

242. Ibid.

243. *OR*, vol. 39, 1: 89, 217, 225.

244. Sherman refused to believe that Sturgis was beaten by a larger Confederate army. On June 16, 1864, Sherman wrote to Washburn, "It is all nonsense about Sturgis being attacked by 15,000 or 20,000. He was whipped by a force inferior to his own. Let the matter be critically investigated." *OR*, vol. 39, 2: 124; Bearss. *Forrest at Brice's Crossroads*, 134.

245. *OR*, vol. 39, 1: 95, 220, 230–31.

246. Ibid., vol. 39, 2: 115, 123, 130.

247. George, "Brice's Cross Roads."

Bibliography

Agnew, Samuel Andrew. "The Battle of Tishomingo Creek: Brice's Cross Roads June 10, 1864." Reprinted for *Baldwyn News*, June 18, 1970, 2.

Bailey, S.J. "Guntown: The Disaster as a Cavalryman Saw It." *National Tribune*, July 12, 1888, 3.

Bartleson, John Wool. Partial diary, Brice's Crossroads Museum and Visitor Center.

Beach, Riley V. *Recollections and Extracts, from Diaries of Army Life from 1862 to 1865 Riley V. Beach, Co. B, 113th Inft, Vols.* N.p.: Terry M. McCarty, 2006.

Bearss, Edwin C. *Forrest at Brice's Crossroads and in North Mississippi in 1864.* Dayton, OH: Morningside Bookshop, 2001.

Bell, Tyree Harris. *Autobiography.* Confederate Veteran Letters. David M. Rubenstein Rare Book & Manuscript Library, Duke University, Raleigh, North Carolina.

Brice, Martha E. Interview, "Brice's Cross Roads: The Battle, June 10, 1864." Ruth Thompson Private Collection, n.d.

Brooksher, William Riley. *Bloody Hill: The Civil War Battle of Wilson's Creek.* Washington, D.C.: Brassey, 1995, 222–23, 225.

Brown, W.D. "Guntown or Brice's X Roads Fight." *Confederate Veteran* 9 (n.d.): 556.

Chamberlain, Samuel. *My Confession: Recollections of a Rogue.* Edited by William H. Goetzmann. Austin: Texas State Historical Association, 1996.

Cogley, Thomas Sydenham. *History of the Seventh Indiana Cavalry Volunteers and the Expeditions, Campaigns, Raids, Marches, and Battles of the Armies with Which*

It Was Connected, with Historical Sketches. LaPorte, IN: Herald Company, Steam Printers, 1876.

Cowden, Robert. *A Brief Sketch of the Organization and Services of the Fifty-Ninth Regiment of United States Colored Infantry.* Dayton, OH: United Brethren Publishing House, 1883.

Dillon, Loyd H. Letter to Dr. G.A. Gessner, March 8, 1882. Dr. Gessner Collection, Hayes Presidential Center, Freemont, Ohio. William Forse Scott. "Roster of the Fourth Iowa Cavalry Veteran Volunteers, 1861–1865," an appendix to *The Story of a Cavalry Regiment*, New York: J.J. Little, 1902.

Dinges, Bruce J., and Shirley A. Leckie, eds. *A Just and Righteous Cause: Benjamin H. Grierson's Civil War Memoir.* Carbondale: Southern Illinois University Press, 2008.

George, Henry. "Brice's Cross Roads: A Visit to One of Gen. Forrest's Triumphant Battle Fields." Brice's Crossroads Visitor Center Collection, 3.

———. *History of the 3d, 7th, 8th and 12th Kentucky C.S.A.* Lyndon, KY: Mull-Wathen Historic Press, 1970.

Gessner Collection. Box 3. Compilation of accounts entitled "General Sturgis at Guntown, Miss. (1864)." Interview with Colonel George B. Hoge, March 1, and later published in the *Chicago Tribune*, 61–62.

———. Box 3. Compilation of accounts entitled "General Sturgis at Guntown, Miss. (1864)." Letter to Chaplain William S. Post, June 30, 1864, and later published in the *Missouri Democrat*, from Dr. L. Dyer, 81st Illinois Infantry Regiment.

———. Box 3. Compilation of accounts entitled "General Sturgis at Guntown, Miss. (1864)." Letter to the *Chicago Tribune* from Reuben L. Sidwell, February 28, year unknown, 60–61.

———. Box 3. Compilation of accounts entitled "General Sturgis at Guntown, Miss. (1864)." Letter to the *Cleveland Leader* from P.C. Smith, February 10, 1882, 39–40.

———. Box 3. Compilation of accounts entitled "General Sturgis at Guntown, Miss. (1864)." Letter to the editor, *Cleveland Leader*, January 9, 1882, from J. Barber, 95th Ohio Infantry Regiment, 17.

———. Box 3. Compilation of accounts entitled "General Sturgis at Guntown, Miss. (1864)." Letter to the editor, *Toledo Blade* from H. Ramsey, March 24, 1879, 4.

———. Box 3. Compilation of accounts entitled "General Sturgis at Guntown, Miss. (1864)." Letter to G.A. Gessner from D.W.C. Thomas, February 9, 1882, 60.

————. Box 3. Compilation of accounts entitled "General Sturgis at Guntown, Miss. (1864)." Letter to G.A. Gessner from J.C. Allen, February 5, 1882, 27.

————. Box 3. Compilation of accounts entitled "General Sturgis at Guntown, Miss. (1864)." Letter to G.A. Gessner from John W. Jenkins, January 24, 1882, 32.

————. Box 3. Compilation of accounts entitled "General Sturgis at Guntown, Miss. (1864)." Letter to G.A. Gessner from R.B. Thrapp, February 13, 1882, 51–52.

————. Box 3. Compilation of accounts entitled "General Sturgis at Guntown, Miss. (1864)." Letter to G.A. Gessner from William Roarke, January 15, 1882, 43.

————. Box 3. Compilation of accounts entitled "General Sturgis at Guntown, Miss. (1864)." Letter to Rev. Wm. S. Post, DD, chaplain with the 81st Illinois Infantry, and later published in the *Missouri Democrat* from Dr. L. Dyer, June 30, 1864, 47–49.

————. Box 3. Compilation of accounts entitled "General Sturgis at Guntown, Miss. (1864)." Letter to the *Toledo Blade*, February 17, 1879, and later published on March 6, 1879, in the *Toledo Blade*, from Lieutenant Colonel E.M. Lowe of the U.S. Colored Troops.

————. Box 3. Compilation of accounts entitled "General Sturgis at Guntown, Miss. (1864)." Letter to wife from soldier in the 114th Illinois Infantry and printed in the *Journal*, n.d., 56–57.

————. Letter from James H. White, Company H, 3rd Iowa Cavalry, to G.A. Gessner, February 8, 1881.

————. Letter from J.H. Mooney, February 20, 1882, Company E, 113th Illinois Infantry Regiment.

————. Letter from John M. Magner to G.A. Gessner, March 7, 1882, Company I, 55th United States Colored Troops.

————. Letter of Captain Eldred Huff, February 20, 1882, Company A, 4th Iowa Cavalry.

————. Letter of Private Joseph McCaulley, February 20, 1882, Company E, 3rd Iowa Cavalry, Logan, *Roster and Record of Iowa Soldiers in the War of the Rebellion Together with Historical Sketches of Volunteer Organizations 1861–1865.* Vol. 4, 549.

————. Letter of R.S. Patten to G.A. Gessner, March 7, 1882, Company B, 114th Illinois Infantry.

————. Letter of Sergeant Charles W. Sherman, Company K, 3rd Iowa Cavalry, Logan, *Roster and Record of Iowa Soldiers in the War of the Rebellion*

Together with Historical Sketches of Volunteer Organizations 1861–1865. Vol. 4, 603.

Gould, Joseph. *The Story of the Forty-eighth: A Record of the Campaigns of the Forty-eighth Regiment Pennsylvania Veteran Volunteer Infantry During the Four Eventful Years of Its Service in the War for the Preservation of the Union.* Philadelphia: Regimental Association, 1908.

Grant, Ulysses S. *Personal Memoirs of U.S. Grant.* 2 vols. New York: Charles L. Webster & Company, 1892.

Hagemann, E.R. *Fighting Rebels and Redskins: Experiences in Army Life of Colonel George B. Sanford 1861–1892.* Norman: University of Oklahoma Press, 1969.

Hall, Russell S. "Sergeant Columbus K. Hall: First Recipient of the Confederate Roll of Honor Medal." *Confederate Veteran* (March–April 2010).

Hancock, Richard R. *Hancock's Diary: or, A History of the Second Tennessee Confederate Cavalry.* Nashville, TN: Brandon Printing Company, 1887.

Haupt, Herman. *Reminiscences of General Herman Haupt.* Milwaukee, WI: Wright & Joys Co., 1901.

Henry, Robert Selph, ed. *As They Saw Forrest: Some Recollections and Comments of Contemporaries.* Jackson, TN: McCowat-Mercer Press, Inc., n.d.

———. *First with the Most: Forrest.* New York: Bobbs-Merrill Company, 1944.

Hills, Parker. "A Study in Warfighting: Nathan Bedford Forrest and the Battle of Brice's Crossroads." *Papers of the Blue and Gray Society*, no. 2 (Fall 1995).

Hord, Henry. "Brice's X Roads from a Private's View." *Confederate Veteran* 529 (n.d.).

Hubbard, John Milton. *Notes of a Private: Company E, 7th Tennessee Regiment, Forrest's Cavalry Corps, C.S.A.* Memphis, TN: E.H. Clarke & Brother, 1909.

Hughes, Nathaniel Cheairs, Jr. *Brigadier General Tyree H. Bell, C.S.A.: Forrest's Fighting Lieutenant.* Knoxville: University of Tennessee Press, 2004.

Johnson, Robert V., Clarence C. Buel and E. Hunn Hanson. "Forrest's Defeat of Sturgis at Brice's Crossroads" (June 10th, 1864). *Battles and Leaders of the Civil War.* New York: The Century Co., 1888.

Johnston, Joseph Eggleston. *Narrative of Military Operations Directed During the Late War Between the States.* New York: D. Appleton and Company, 1874.

Jordan, Thomas, and J.P. Pryor. *The Campaigns of Lieut-Gen. N.B. Forrest.* New Orleans, LA: Blelock & Company, 1868.

Lacock, John W. "The Guntown Trip: One of the Disastrous Blunders of the War." *National Tribune*, June 16, 1887, 1.

Lee, Stephen D. *Battle of Brice's Crossroads, or Tishomingo Creek, June 2nd to 12th, 1864*. Edited by Franklin L. Riley. Oxford: Publications of the Mississippi Historical Society, 1902, 27–28.

Logan, Guy E. *Roster and Record of Iowa Soldiers in the War of the Rebellion Together with Historical Sketches of Volunteer Organizations 1861–1865*. Des Moines, IA: Emory H. English, State Printer, E.D. Chassel, State Binder, 1910.

Lowe, E.M. "At Guntown: What the Colored Troops Did There." *National Tribune*, December 29, 1887, 3.

MacDonald, Colin F. "The Battle of Brice's Cross Roads." In *Papers of the Military Order of the Loyal Legion of the United States*. 56 vols. Minneapolis, MN: Aug. Davis, Publisher, 1909.

Marsh. Letter to "My Dear Brother John," October 11, 1864, 55th United States Colored Troops, file in Brice's Crossroads Visitor Center Collection, Baldwyn, Mississippi.

Mathes, James Harvey. *General Forrest*. New York: D. Appleton and Company, 1902.

Maury, Dabney Herndon. *Recollections of a Virginian in the Mexican, Indian, and Civil War*. New York: Charles Scribner's Sons, 1894.

McCarty, Terry M., and Margaret Ann Chatfield McCarty, eds. *The Chatfield Story: Civil War Letters and Diaries of Private Edward L. Chatfield of the 113th Illinois Volunteers*. North Charleston, SC: BookSurge Publishing, 2009.

Minnesota Board of Commissioners. *Minnesota in the Civil and Indian Wars 1861–1865*, St. Paul, MN: Pioneer Press Company, 1893.

Morton, John Watson. *The Artillery of Nathan Bedford Forrest's Cavalry*. Nashville, TN: Publishing House of the M.E. Church, South Smith & Lamar, Agents, 1909.

Newsom, Edmund. Letter to Dr. G.A. Gessner, February 21, 1882. Dr. Gessner Collection, Hayes Presidential Center.

O'Reilly, Francis Augustin. *The Fredericksburg Campaign: Winter War on the Rappahannock*. Baton Rouge: Louisiana State University Press, 2003.

Orr, James H. "Guntown Again: The Conflict of June 10, 1864." *National Tribune*, January 5, 1888, 1.

Reece, J.N. *Report of the Adjutant General of the State of Illinois*. Springfield, IL: Journal Company, Printers and Binders, 1900.

Scott, William Forse. *The Story of a Cavalry Regiment: The Career of the Fourth Iowa Veteran Volunteers from Kansas to Georgia 1861–1865*. New York: G.T. Putnam's Sons, 1893.

Sherman, William T. *Memoirs of W.T. Sherman*. New York: Charles L. Webster & Co., 1892.

Skaptason, Bjorn, ed. "West Tennessee U.S. Colored Troops and the Retreat from Brice's Crossroads: An Eyewitness Account by Major James C. Foster (USA)." *West Tennessee Historical Society Papers* 50 (2007).

U.S. War Department. *The War of the Rebellion: A Compilation of the Official Records of the Union and Confederate Armies*. 128 vols. Washington, D.C.: Government Printing Office, 1880–1901.

Waring, George E. *Whip and Spur*. New York: Doubleday and McClure Company, 1897.

Warner, Ezra J. *Generals in Blue: Lives of the Union Commanders*. Baton Rouge: Louisiana State University Press, n.d.

———. *Generals in Gray: Lives of the Confederate Commanders*. Baton Rouge: Louisiana State University Press, n.d.

Waugh, John G. *The Class of 1846 from West Point to Appomattox: Stonewall Jackson, George McClellan and Their Brothers*. New York: Time Warner, 1994.

Welsh, Jack D. *Medical Histories of Union Generals*. Kent, OH: Kent State University Press, 1996.

Wilkin, Alexander. Letter, "Dear Sarah," Memphis, Tennessee, June 18, 1864. Alexander Wilkin Collection. The St. Paul Insurance Companies, St. Paul, Minnesota.

Wills, Brian Steel. *A Battle from the Start*. New York: HarperCollins, 1992.

Witherspoon, William. *Tishomingo Creek or Bryce's Cross Roads As I Saw It*. Jackson, TN: published by the author, 1906.

Wood, Wales W. *A History of the Ninety-Fifth Regiment Illinois Infantry Volunteers*, Chicago: Tribune Company's Book and Job Printing Office, 1865.

Wyeth, John Allen. *Life of General Nathan Bedford Forrest*. New York: Harper & Bros., 1899.

———. *Life of Lieutenant-General Nathan Bedford Forrest*. New York: Harper & Brothers Publishers, 1908.

Young, John Preston. *The Seventh Tennessee Cavalry, Confederate, A History*. Nashville, TN: Publishing House of the M.E. Church, 1890.

Index

A

Agnew, Samuel A. 45, 112, 113,
    114, 118, 122
Allen, J.C. 121
Andersonville 121, 122
Atlanta 12, 13, 14, 15, 20, 124
Atlanta Campaign 15, 16, 22

B

Baldwyn, Mississippi 30, 36, 37,
    38, 41, 43, 56, 57, 63, 64
Baldwyn road 42, 43, 44, 45, 46,
    50, 52, 54, 59, 64, 71, 73, 94,
    95
Barteau, Colonel C.R. 72, 95, 97,
    98, 107, 108, 129
Bartleson, John Wool 33, 90, 92,
    102
Battle of Buena Vista 17
Battle of Chickamauga 20
Battle of Fredericksburg 19
Battle of Murfreesboro 88

Battle of Shiloh 20, 121
Battle of Tishomingo Creek 37
Battle of Wilson's Creek 18
Beach, Riley V. 94, 95, 100
Bellamy, William 92
Bell, Captain John E. 77
Bell, Colonel Tyree H. 42, 43,
    46, 47, 51, 65, 71, 72, 76,
    77, 78, 79, 85, 86, 88, 89,
    99, 100, 104, 114, 129, 133,
    138, 139
Bell, Isaac T. 78
Bolivar, Tennessee 20, 21, 22
Booneville, Mississippi 30, 35, 36,
    43
Bouton, Colonel Edward 26, 31,
    66, 69, 100, 104, 106, 107,
    110, 119, 128, 140
Bragg, General Braxton 11, 14,
    20
Browne, Lt. Colonel Thomas M.
    53, 54, 128
Brown, Lieutenant W.D. 46, 101,
    117

Brumback, Lieutenant Colonel
    Jefferson 95, 103, 127
Buford, Brigadier General
    Abraham 29, 30, 35, 36, 37,
    42, 43, 46, 65, 71, 76, 86, 88,
    98, 129, 138
Bush, Captain E.N. 93
Bush, Captain E.W. 127

C

Campbell, Colonel Franklin 68, 90,
    92, 127
Canby, Major General 25, 26
Chalmers, Lieutenant Colonel A.H.
    38, 130
Chapman, Captain F.H. 26, 66,
    128
Chatfield, Private Edward L. 22,
    33
Chattanooga, Tennessee 11, 13,
    14, 20
Clarke, Lieutenant Colonel George
    R. 67
Cogley, 1st Lieutenant Thomas S.
    11, 31, 53, 54
Corinth, Mississippi 25, 26, 27, 30,
    32, 42
Cowden, Lieutenant Colonel
    Robert 69, 111, 128

D

Dalton, Georgia 11, 22
Davis, President Jefferson 14
Decatur, Alabama 16, 26
Dillon, 2nd Lieutenant Loyd H. 18
Doan, Captain J.F. 130
Donaldson, Captain Sam 37

Dry Creek 113, 114
Duckworth, Colonel W.L. 130
Duff, Colonel W.L. 130
Dyer, Dr. L. 68, 118

E

Eaton, Lt. Colonel Charles G. 96,
    109, 127
Ewing, Captain 106, 109

F

Fernald, Captain 75
Ferrero, General Edward 19
Fitch, Captain John A. 103, 127
Floyd, Lt. Colonel S.B. 128
Forrest, Major General Nathan
    Bedford 13, 14, 16, 19, 20,
    21, 22, 23, 25, 26, 27, 29, 30,
    35, 36, 37, 38, 42, 43, 44, 46,
    47, 51, 52, 56, 63, 64, 66, 71,
    72, 76, 78, 80, 84, 86, 88, 95,
    98, 99, 101, 102, 103, 107,
    110, 111, 112, 114, 115, 118,
    120, 121, 122, 123, 124, 125,
    129, 133, 134, 136, 138
Fort Donaldson 20
Fort Pickering 121
Fort Pillow 20, 104, 117
Foster, Major James C. 41, 128

G

Gayoso House 28
George, Henry 125
Gessner, Dr. Gustavus A. 144
Grant, Major General Ulysses S.
    11, 12, 16

Grierson, Brigadier General
    Benjamin H. 26, 28, 31, 32,
    34, 37, 38, 41, 42, 46, 49, 51,
    56, 62, 63, 64, 65, 66, 67, 78,
    79, 83, 98, 100, 103, 109,
    112, 123, 128, 134, 136, 137,
    139

H

Hall, Sgt. Columbus K. 88
Hancock, Richard R. 35, 42, 138
Hanson, Major Robert N. 43, 50,
    53, 56
Hatchie Bottom 42, 62, 66, 67, 69,
    110, 111, 114, 118, 119
Haupt, Colonel Herman 18
Hess, Lt. Colonel J.C. 128
Hill, Ambrose Powell 17
Hill, Tom 92
Hoge, Colonel George B. 26, 31,
    34, 66, 67, 68, 73, 75, 86, 88,
    89, 98, 100, 127
Holly Springs, Mississippi 25
Holt, Lt. Colonel G.A.C. 129
Hord, Private Henry 45, 62, 101,
    107
Hubbard, Private John Milton 61,
    73, 88
Huff, Captain Eldred 62
Humphrey, Colonel T.W. 67, 93,
    127
Hurlbut, Major General S.A. 15

I

Indian Wars 17

J

Jackson, Mississippi 21
Jackson, Thomas "Stonewall" 17
Jenkins, John W. 76
Johnson, Colonel William A. 37,
    42, 46, 51, 53, 56, 72, 77, 86,
    88, 97, 98, 102, 108, 130
Johnston, Major General Joseph E.
    12, 13, 14, 19, 22, 23, 25, 52,
    124
Jones, Major 60

K

King, Lt. Colonel John F. 84, 85,
    114, 127

L

Lafayette, Tennessee 30, 31, 33
LaGrange, Tennessee 33
Lamberg, Captain C.A. 110, 128
Lee, Lt. General Robert E. 12
Lee, Major General Stephen Dill
    14, 23, 29, 30, 36, 37, 38,
    119, 124, 129, 131, 133
Lincoln, President Abraham 11, 125
Little Dry Creek 113
Louisville, Kentucky 13
Lowe, Major Edgar M. 106, 110,
    128, 134, 140, 143
Lundy's Lane 16
Lyon, Brigadier General Nathaniel
    18
Lyon, Colonel Hylan B. 38, 42, 43,
    44, 45, 51, 52, 53, 54, 55, 62,
    72, 86, 93, 98, 103, 118, 125,
    129

M

Mallory, Captain Egbert O. 111
Marsh, Lt. Colonel J.F. 81, 82, 117, 127
Maury, Dabney Herndon 17
McCaulley, Private Joseph 61
McClellan, George B. 17
McClure, Lieutenant 38
McKeaig, Colonel G.W. 128
McMillen, Colonel William L. 20, 26, 31, 34, 41, 63, 66, 67, 73, 74, 75, 78, 81, 86, 89, 95, 98, 100, 101, 103, 106, 108, 109, 110, 111, 114, 119, 127
McPherson, Major General James B. 15, 16, 20, 23, 26, 121, 124, 127
Meade, Major General George Gordan 12
Memphis and Charleston Railroad 27
Memphis, Tennessee 15, 16, 19, 20, 21, 22, 23, 25, 26, 27, 28, 29, 30, 33, 34, 35, 38, 118, 119, 120, 121, 122, 124
Missionary Ridge 11, 14
Mobile & Ohio Railroad 37
Mock, Captain A.A. 128, 135
Montgomery, Alabama 15
Mooney, J.H. 67, 93, 94
Moore, Captain 53
Morgan, General John Hunt 14
Mower, General 125
Mueller, Captain M. 75, 97, 127

N

Nashville, Tennessee 13, 16, 29
Newsom, Colonel J.F. 129
Noble, Lt. Colonel John W. 62

O

Okolona, Mississippi 26, 30, 37, 38, 42, 134
Old Carrollville, Mississippi 43, 138
Orr, James H. 91

P

Pickett, George Edward 17
Pierce, Major Abial R. 75, 108, 128
Pike, Lieutenant 38
Polk, Lt. General Leonidas 21
Pontotoc, Mississippi 37
Pontotoc road 47, 57, 78, 102
Poole, Lt. Colonel 79, 81
Pope, General John 18

R

Randle, Captain 43, 44
Rawolle, Captain 64
Reeves, Captain A.T. 128
Reno, Jesse Lee 17
Rice, Captain T.W. 30, 43, 71, 114, 115, 123, 130
Rienzi, Mississippi 30, 42
Ripley, Mississippi 21, 29, 32, 33, 34, 35, 36, 37, 45, 49, 65, 72, 75, 77, 79, 102, 103, 104,

107, 109, 110, 112, 113, 114, 118, 120, 121, 122, 138

Roarke, William 76

Roddey, Brigadier General 29, 63

Rogers, Lt. Colonel Andrew W. 92, 127

Roll of Honor 88

Rucker, Colonel Edmund 36, 37, 38, 42, 46, 51, 52, 54, 55, 60, 61, 62, 71, 72, 86, 88, 89, 93, 100, 104, 130

Ruckersville, Mississippi 32, 35

Russell, Colonel R.M. 129

Russell, J.B. 120

S

Sale, Lieutenant T. Saunders 130

Salem, Mississippi 30, 32

Santa Fe, New Mexico 17

Sedgwick, Major John 17

Selma, Alabama 15

Shackett, Lt. Colonel A.R. 129

Shellenberger, Captain A. 127

Sherman, Major General William T. 12, 13, 14, 15, 16, 19, 20, 22, 23, 26, 29, 30, 120, 124, 125, 145

Sherrill, Lt. Colonel L.J. 129

Sidwell, Lt. Colonel Reuben L. 93, 128

Sigel, Colonel Franz 18

Smith, A.J. 26, 123, 124

Stanton, Edwin M. 124

Stewart, Captain William H. 127

Stubb's farm 36, 38, 41, 45

Sturgis, Brevet Capatain William 16

Sturgis, Brigadier General Samuel D. 16, 17, 18, 19, 20, 21, 22, 23, 25, 26, 27, 28, 29, 30, 31, 32, 33, 34, 35, 36, 37, 38, 41, 42, 47, 56, 57, 62, 63, 64, 65, 66, 67, 69, 78, 79, 83, 89, 93, 100, 101, 102, 103, 104, 109, 110, 111, 112, 114, 118, 119, 120, 121, 122, 123, 127, 132, 134, 137, 139, 140, 145

T

Tate, Major T.S. 129

Tennessee River 16, 19, 20, 29, 30

Terry, Captain F.C. 43

Thomas, Colonel DeWitt C. 31, 42, 127

Tishomingo Creek 11, 47, 48, 56, 73, 75, 78, 83, 96, 98, 99, 100, 102, 107, 112, 113, 125, 126

Tupelo, Mississippi 21, 25, 26, 29, 30, 34, 43, 124

Twenty-mile Creek 35

Tyler, Captain Henry A. 44, 71, 72, 78, 80, 81, 82, 99, 102, 104

V

Vicksburg 11, 20, 121

von Heimrich, Lt. Colonel G. 128

W

Ward, Colonel L.M. 28

Waring, Colonel George E., Jr. 20, 25, 26, 50, 53, 54, 55, 56, 65, 66, 73, 75, 76, 79, 112, 128, 135

War of 1812 16

Warren, Captain W.H. 130

Washburn, Major General
Cadwallader C. 15, 19, 20,
21, 22, 23, 25, 26, 27, 29, 35,
120, 124, 127, 145

Western and Atlantic Railroad 13

White House Ridge 110, 111, 114,
118

White, Private James H. 56

Wilkin, Colonel Alexander 31, 66,
68, 82, 96, 111, 113, 115,
118, 119, 127, 140

Williams, Major M.H. 128

Wilson, Colonel A.N. 129

Windes, Lt. Colonel F.M. 130

Witherspoon, William 60

Wolf Creek 35

Wood, Wales W. 93

Woodward, Captain S.L. 34, 38

About the Author

Stewart Bennett attended Grace College and graduated with a bachelor's degree in behavioral science. He received his master of arts degree from Youngstown State University and his doctor of philosophy degree in interdisciplinary studies in history and political science from the University of Maine. He is the co-editor of the work *The Struggle for the Life of the Republic: A Civil War Narrative by Brevet Major Charles Dana Miller, 76th Ohio Volunteer Infantry.* Stewart is the department chair of social and behavior sciences and assistant professor of history at Blue Mountain College in Blue Mountain, Mississippi.

Visit us at
www.historypress.net